KEEP ON
KEEPING ON

KEEP ON
KEEPING ON

How to Stay Faithful Serving God

Leslie B. Flynn

MAGNUS PRESS

MAGNUS PRESS
P.O. Box 2666
Carlsbad, CA 92018

www.magnuspress.com

Keep On Keeping On

First Edition, 2005

Printed in the United States of America

All Scripture quotations, unless otherwise noted, are taken from the HOLY BIBLE, NEW INTERNATIONAL VERSION®. Copyright © 1973, 1978, 1984 by International Bible Society. Used by permission of International Bible Society.

LCCN: 2004110888
ISBN: 0-9724869-2-5

Publisher's Cataloging-in-Publication
(Prepared by The Donohue Group, Inc.)

Flynn, Leslie B.
    Keep on keeping on : how to stay faithful serving God / by Leslie B. Flynn. — 1st ed. —

        p. ;   cm.
        ISBN: 0-9724869-2-5
1. Clergy—Office. 2. Christian life.
3. Inspiration—Religious aspects—Christianity.
I. Title.

BV660.2 .F59 2005
253   2004110888

---

10 09 08 07 06 05   10 9 8 7 6 5 4 3 2 1

To my wife Bernice

who keeps on exercising her gift of exhortation

in correspondence and in personal contact,

especially in the repeated urging of friends

to write for publication.

At the beginning of my public ministry and our married life,

she challenged me to think beyond the preaching of the

word over the sacred desk

to the ministry of writing articles and books.

This book is a result of her strong encouragement.

From the Author...

The Story of Dr. Ralph and
Carolyn Partelow

On their first wedding anniversary, Carolyn Partelow was diagnosed with multiple sclerosis. Despite this setback, the Partelows accepted a church in Pennsylvania where they had a rewarding and fruitful ministry. They were also told that Carolyn could never bear children. Yet six years later Jonathan was born, their "miracle child."

During their pastoral ministry they felt God's call for Ralph to further his education and consider the mission field. At a friend's suggestion they applied to the African Inland Mission (AIM) and were accepted, but they needed to raise thousands of dollars for equipment within a year. Where would the money come from?

Music and musical instruments had intrigued Ralph since he was twelve years old. This interest sparked his hobby of making miniature pianos, for which he is now well known. John H. Steinway of Steinway & Sons piano company encouraged him. Articles about his creations appeared in the *New York Times* and leading miniature magazines. Constant orders for the pianos began arriving, enabling them to leave for Africa debt free. In Africa, Ralph taught at Scott Theological College. Carolyn served as a prayer warrior, and exercised her gift of hospitality. They traveled back and forth from Africa six times to treat Carolyn's medical problems and enable Ralph to earn his Doctor of Ministry degree from Denver Seminary. While stateside, Ralph pastored several churches, but the call to Africa never abated.

Their last six months in Africa were especially difficult. As Ralph described it, life-threatening muggings, armed robberies, illnesses, and a head-on collision (caused by a reckless driver in a no-passing zone) all took their toll.

Before they left Africa in 2003, the president of Kenya came in full regalia accompanied by his entourage to pay a visit to the Partelows. In a public announcement, he said he had come to see the lady who had prayed for him daily for twenty-four years. Now living in Pearl River, New York, Ralph is Missionary Relations Administrator at AIM, which involves the overall care of AIM missionaries from the United States, who serve all over Africa. He lovingly cares for Carolyn, who needs help with eating and dressing. She goes from bed to wheelchair without complaint. Her mind is sharp. She inspires everyone she meets and spends hours praying for the AIM mission needs. For relaxation between his job, caring for Carolyn, and doing all the cooking and cleaning, Ralph continues to make miniature pianos, but only on special order.

Ralph and Carolyn Partelow have spent their lives together demonstrating the ability to *keep on keeping on.* Throughout their hardships they have struggled with questions of why God would allow so many misfortunes to come upon them. But, in their own words, they have been able to accept their trials as opportunities to experience God's grace and power.

Contents

Preface

Since the 1970s Dr. Armand Nicholi Jr. has been teaching a course at Harvard entitled "Sigmund Freud and C. S. Lewis: Two Contrasting Worldviews." Nicholi is Associate Clinical Professor of Psychiatry at Harvard Medical School and has an active practice as a psychiatrist. In the class Nicholi compares what Lewis and Freud had to say about life's most important questions and lets the students come to the truth on the strength of each case made. The class has been so popular that there's room for only one in four of those who sign up. Class material is now available in Nicholi's recent book, *The Question of God: C. S. Lewis and Sigmund Freud Debate God, Love, Sex, and the Meaning of Life* (The Free Press, 2002).

At the end of the book is Nicholi's acknowledgment: "To Dr. Vernon Grounds, who first encouraged my interest in the field of psychiatry and who, over the years, sent me a continuous flow of articles and books to focus my attention on writing this one." Dr. Grounds is the former president and present chancellor of Denver Seminary.

When I mentioned this acknowledgment to Grounds, he replied, "I had no idea Nicholi was writing this book. Though I did indeed encourage him every now and again, the book was a total surprise as was the acknowledgment. I didn't learn about the acknowledgment until after the book came out and a friend told me about it."

I asked Grounds about his contacts with Nicholi. He said, "I became acquainted with him when I served on the faculty of Baptist Bible Seminary in Johnson City, New York, from 1945-51. He was an active member of the youth fellowship of the First Baptist Church, already a serious-minded believer. He played football on the high school team. We talked together many times, discussing his future career. He was thinking about medicine, so I urged him to at least consider the possibility of becoming a psychiatrist, saying that we needed Christians in that field. I kept in touch with him through his college years and when he did his necessary training in psychiatry. Every now and again over the years I put in a plug for a book on Sigmund Freud."

Though the appearance of Nicholi's book and its generous acknowledgment caught Grounds off guard, this wasn't his only surprise in connection with Nicholi's book. Gordon College decided to award Nicholi an honorary doctorate at its May 2002 commencement. Because of his relationship with Nicholi, Grounds was invited to attend and offer the prayer after Nicholi received the honorary degree. Nicholi, not informed of Grounds' participation, was shocked when Grounds appeared in the academic procession the morning of the graduation exercises. Nicholi's remarks turned out to be more or less a praise of Grounds who says, "I sat there on the platform while he was at the podium extolling my virtues, and I tried to appear humble. I'm not sure that I succeeded."

Here is the major part of Nicholi's response: "More than anyone else, Dr. Grounds influenced my writing this book, which stems from a course I have been teaching at Harvard College and the Harvard Medical School for several decades.

"Dr. Grounds not only influenced the writing of this book; he influenced my whole career. As a young teenager, growing up in a very small town in upstate New York, I met Dr. Grounds in a church I began attending soon after I had come to personal faith. With uncanny timing, he arrived to head a small seminary, stayed a few years and then left for Denver. But during those few years, he took an interest in me. He suggested I go to college. Most young people went to work at IBM or in shoe factories where their parents worked. Once I decided on college, he suggested I become a doctor. He said we needed more good doctors who were men of faith. He wrote to me often at college, and several times suggested I consider the field of psychiatry.

"Once I entered psychiatry, he continued to write. He thought it would be helpful to many people if I wrote a book on Freud and his worldview from a Christian perspective. He sent me books and letters and quietly and patiently encouraged me for more than thirty years. He played a role in the courses I ended up teaching. The courses led to my being invited to give the Noble Lectures at Harvard; the lectures, in turn, finally led to this book. So let me leave you with this thought. Now that you are leaving college, seek out a good mentor. Our mentor may be someone who suddenly appears in our life at a time when we need that person most, often with uncanny timing, sent by Someone who has promised that if we acknowledge Him in all our ways, He will direct our paths."

I asked Dr. Grounds a second time about his awareness through those more than thirty years of the sway his life had exerted on Nicholi's career and book. Again Grounds affirmed, "I had no idea I was being such an influence."

May not Grounds' experience be a miniature foreshadowing of a coming judgment day when the Lord rolls back the curtain and shows believers how, all unknown to them, they were a major factor in the important decisions of someone else's life? What a surprise and delight for faithful believers to find out on that day of reckoning that the way we lived, and what we said, made an indelible influence in the lives of others!

This concept applies not only to mentoring, but also to the whole host of good works which believers are exhorted to do. Many kind deeds, here unnoticed and unsung, there will be openly revealed and divinely rewarded. And many doers of good who thought their efforts were fruitless and useless will learn that they vitally impacted the lives of others, and will receive recognition and commendation. Someone in heaven will say, "You're the reason I'm here." Or, "Because of you, I was able to feed my children," or "I served on the mission field," or "I regained my health," or "I came back to the Lord and to church."

This book will explore the text, "Let us not become weary in doing good, for at the proper time we will reap a harvest if we do not give up" (Galatians 6:9). We will deal with the doing of good, the danger of weariness and discouragement, and the delight of a guaranteed harvest, even though delayed, for those resolved not to quit.

So let's *keep on keeping on!*

Leslie B. Flynn
Nanuet, New York

Chapter 1

The Importance of Good Works

On the morning of the infamous September 11, Todd Beamer was flying from Newark to San Francisco on United Airlines Flight 93 when the plane was taken over by hijackers. Trying to call his wife of seven years, he was intercepted by a GTE operator, who informed him of the Twin Towers and Pentagon disasters. Beamer immediately suspected that the hijackers planned to use his flight to strike some important Washington, D.C. target and kill significant numbers on the ground. He and other passengers in the rear of the plane decided to try to stop the hijackers any way they could.

Just before they charged down the plane's aisle, Beamer and the operator recited the 23d Psalm together. Exactly what happened before the plane crashed in Pennsylvania may never be fully known, but the last words the operator heard from Beamer was a charge to his fellow passengers, "Let's roll!" It was a charge he had given many times to his family and exemplified his enthusiastic spirit.

President Bush and the nation gratefully recognized that the sacrifice of those who tried to overpower the hijackers probably saved the White House from tragedy that day. Beamer's hometown area of Cranberry, New Jersey, recognized his bravery and resolve in a public ceremony on May 4, 2002, when they officially renamed their local mail center the "Todd Beamer Post Office."

Todd Beamer, a Christian, did a "good work." His act probably ranks ultimate in the hierarchy of good works. The apostle John wrote in what has been called the other John 3:16, "Jesus Christ laid down his life for us. And we ought to lay down our lives for our brothers" (1 John 3:16). Most of us will not be called on to make that supreme sacrifice. However, the Bible repeatedly exhorts us to do a myriad of less spectacular good works. The next verse carries this pointed reminder, "If anyone has material possessions and sees his brother in need but has no pity on him, how can the love of God be in him? Dear children, let us not love with words or tongue but with actions and in truth" (vs. 17-18).

Not only are we ordered to do good works, but we are commanded to keep on doing them to the end of life. We are familiar with the apostle Paul's urging, "Let us not become weary in doing good, for at the proper time we will reap a harvest if we do not give up" (Gal. 6:9). This book is a commentary on this text, dealing with such concepts as the doing of good, the characteristics of a good work, the danger of weariness, the deadliness of discouragement, the sureness of the harvest, the possibility of a delayed harvest, the resolve to persevere, and some keys to keep from quitting. Most of all, it shows us how we can stay faithful in serving God all our lives.

IS DOING GOOD THE WAY TO HEAVEN?

I had the wonderful privilege of growing up in a gospel-preaching, Bible-teaching, missionary-oriented church. And one emphasis that came across very vividly was that we are *not* saved by doing good. This downplay of works was a reaction against salvation-by-character theology in which some people believe that entrance to heaven depends on good behavior. Many reason that at life's end all our deeds are placed on a scale, and if the good outweighs the bad we'll be saved, but if the bad outbalances the good we'll be lost. When a person passes away, how often we hear, "Oh, she's up in heaven. She was such a good person."

To counter this prevalent but mistaken belief, the church leaders of my youth frequently and emphatically quoted Ephesians 2:8-9, "For it is by grace you have been saved, through faith—and this not from yourselves, it is the gift of God—not by works, so that no one can boast." And we were required to memorize it!

They also piled on Titus 3:4-5a, "But when the kindness and love of God our Savior appeared, he saved us, not because of righteous things we had done, but because of his mercy." How often I heard speakers refer disparagingly to those trying to gain heaven by their good works as "do-gooders." Our teachers listed these following questions to ask people who depend on their own goodness to merit heaven.

(1) If heaven can be earned by good deeds, why did Jesus tell us that we needed the new birth to enter God's kingdom? Nicodemus was a good man, a religious leader, a member of the Sanhedrin, a doer of good works, a model worthy of emulation, yet Jesus told this good man three times, "You must be born again."

(2) If good deeds earn heaven, how did the thief on the cross get there? In his dying hours, he was unable to stretch out his hand to do one simple, good thing. But because it's not by works, but by faith in the Savior, he turned to Jesus and

asked him, "Jesus, remember me when you come into your kingdom." Jesus response was immediate, "Today you will be with me in paradise"—no strings attached, no good works required. Doubtless, had the thief lived, his good deeds would have been many.

(3) If a person can earn his way to heaven, why did Jesus die? Jesus came to pay the penalty for our sins through his death on the cross. We could charge God with the utmost cruelty for sending his son to the agonies of Calvary, had there been any other way to forgive us. It's trusting Jesus that counts, not doing good. We need him as our Savior first before we try to follow him as our example.

(4) What song would people sing up in heaven if they were depending on their good works to get them there? Up there they sing to the Lamb, "You are worthy...because you were slain, and with your blood you purchased men for God" (Rev. 5:9). People would be so out of place and embarrassed trying to sing, "Unto myself who am worthy because I have done so many good deeds," while all around you redeemed throngs were singing, "Worthy is the Lamb."

So many religions of the world make good works the way to salvation. For example, the "Five Pillars" define the duties of every Muslim. They are: at least one pilgrimage to Mecca, fasting, almsgiving, ritual prayer five times a day facing Mecca, and recitation of the creed that there is no god but Allah and Muhammad is his prophet. By performing these works in the prescribed manner Muslims earn merit for the scales of judgment on which their good works and bad works will be weighed.

Someone said that Christianity can be distinguished from all other religions by the words, "do" and "done." Religions say, "Do. Do good. Do good works. This is the way to win God's forgiveness." But the Christian faith says that our forgiveness is a "done" thing, an accomplished fact. When Jesus was about to die, one of his last words was, "It is finished." He had accomplished our redemption. Jesus paid it all. Salvation is a gift for which we cannot work, but can only receive. As one hymnwriter put it, "Nothing in my hand I bring, Simply to thy cross I cling."

When Chuck Colson resigned the presidency of Prison Fellowship, which he had founded, former Virginia attorney general Mark Earley was commissioned as the new president. Earley gave this testimony: "I came from a tremendous family. We went to a little Methodist church across the street from my house every Sunday. Growing up I had a very positive perception of who God was. My understanding of what it meant to be a Christian was to keep the Ten Commandments, be good, obey my parents, work hard in school, be nice to other people. And at the end of my life, if I were good enough, I'd go to heaven. That's not a bad thing for a kid to want to do, but it wasn't the Good News of Jesus Christ. I hadn't heard the gospel yet in a way that I really understood."

Earley tells how in his senior year he had a new Sunday school teacher who had just become a Christian and who led a Bible study through the Gospel of John. When they reached John 3:16 he had Earley read it out loud, putting his name in it. A little embarrassed, he read it: "For God so loved Mark Earley, that he gave his only begotten Son, that if Mark Earley believes in him, Mark Earley will not perish, but have everlasting life." This opened the door for Earley to understand how Jesus died on the cross for him personally. One night, just before retiring, Earley got down on his knees and asked Jesus to be his Savior and Lord.

Those who trust in their own goodness are trying to be their own savior. In reality they are ignoring Jesus Christ as their rightful and only redeemer.

SHOULD WE BELITTLE GOOD WORKS?

Earlier I mentioned my upbringing in a Bible-teaching church with its emphasis on the inability of good works to earn God's saving favor. I will ever be grateful for this teaching of the old, old story of Jesus' free forgiveness apart from human merit. But as the years went by, especially those in Bible school, college, and seminary, I began to see the other side of the coin that perhaps had been understressed, or that I had missed.

I came to realize that believers are repeatedly told to abound in the doing of good works.

It suddenly dawned on me one day that the two classic verses I had had to memorize in evangelism class debunking salvation by works were immediately followed by commands to believers to *do* good deeds. For example, Ephesians 2:8-9, which emphatically tells us that salvation is by grace and not by works, is followed by v.10, which says, "For we are God's workmanship, created in Christ Jesus to do good works, which God prepared in advance for us to do." Though good works can never earn salvation, those who come to Christ to receive the gift of salvation are commanded to perform them thereafter. God's purpose in saving us is to conform us to the likeness of Jesus.

The other verse, Titus 3:5, tells us that God didn't save us "because of righteous things we had done, but because of his mercy." Then, in the same context, comes a specific instruction from Paul to Titus, "This is a trustworthy saying. And I want you to stress these things, so that those who have trusted in God may be careful to devote themselves to doing what is good. These things are excellent and profitable for everyone" (v. 8). When we become the recipients of forgiveness through the gift of God's mercy, we are obligated to show our appreciation by doing good works.

SOME DOERS OF GOOD IN THE NEW TESTAMENT

Paramount is the example of *Jesus*. When Peter preached the gospel to the household of Cornelius, Peter summarized Jesus' three-year earthly, pre-Calvary ministry simply: "he went around *doing good* and healing all who were under the power of the devil because God was with him" (Acts 10:38, italics mine). If we would be like Jesus, we should be going around doing good in the love of God as Jesus did.

When Mary, the sister of Martha, poured ointment worth a year's wages on Jesus, the disciples thought it a waste. But Jesus, who knew her heart, declared that she did this act of devotion in anticipation of his burial. Somehow she had rightly sensed that the situation of his quick demise would not permit the proper, orderly anointing of his corpse in the Jewish custom.

Jesus commented, "She has done a beautiful thing to me" (Matt. 26:10). The King James puts it, "She hath wrought a good work upon me."

Dorcas, who lived in Joppa, was always doing good by helping the poor and making clothes for the needy with her sanctified needle. The King James says, "This woman was full of good works" (Acts 9:36). Countless churchwomen's societies have immortalized her name.

Whenever Barnabas is mentioned in Acts, he's always help-ing. Because of this characteristic, he was given the name "son of encouragement." He accepted the questionable Gentile believers at Antioch, enlisted a capable assistant to teach them, vouched for the genuineness of Paul when the Jerusalem lead-ers suspicioned his conversion, initiated a relief effort for the famine-stricken Jews of Jerusalem, and sold his own property to feed the hungry. Many other early believers sold land and houses to meet the needs of others (Acts 4:34-35).

When Paul was a prisoner at Rome in his final incarcera-tion (not the first time when in the comfort of his own hired house) in some dank, dark, dungeon-like jail—probably the dreaded Mammertine prison—he was visited by Onesiphorus, of whom he wrote that "he often refreshed me and was not ashamed of my chains. On the contrary, when he was in Rome, he searched hard for me until he found me…. You know very well in how many ways he helped me in Ephesus" (2 Tim. 1:16-18). The name "Onesiphorus" means literally "prof-it-bringer" or "help-bringer" or, in broader terms, "mercy-doer." He was indeed (in deed) a doer of good works.

GOOD WORKS ARE COMMANDED AND COMMENDED

The 3,000 who believed Peter's message at Pentecost not only devoted themselves to the apostles' teaching, fellowship, breaking of bread and prayer, but "had everything in com-mon. Selling their possessions and goods, they gave to anyone as he had need" (Acts 2:42-45). We never hear much about the resolutions of the apostles, but a great deal about their deeds. In fact, the book that follows the four Gospels bears the title Acts of the Apostles and is a continuation "of all that Jesus began *to do* and to teach" (Acts 1:1, italics mine).

In his defense before King Agrippa, Paul told how he preached to Jews and Gentile alike, "that they should repent and turn to God and prove their repentance by their deeds" (Acts 26:20). His message was not one of easy believism, but of genuine do-ism, as a demonstration of their faith. Paul continually reminded his readers to practice good deeds:

(1) to the Romans, "Share with God's people who are in need. Practice hospitality" (12:13).

(2) to the Corinthians, "God is able to make all grace abound to you, so that in all things at all times, having all that you need, you will abound in every good work" (2 Cor. 9:8).

(3) to Timothy, "Command them [those well-off] to do good, to be rich in good deeds, and to be generous and willing to share" (1 Tim. 6:18). Earlier in this same letter Paul had written that a Christian widow should be "well known for her good deeds, such as bringing up children, showing hospitality, washing the feet of the saints, helping those in trouble and devoting herself to all kinds of good deeds" (5:10). Note that good deeds are mentioned twice.

(4) to Titus, he wrote that those redeemed by Jesus should be "eager to do what is good" (2:14). Several other times this letter orders good works (2:7; 3:1, 8, 14).

The author of Hebrews tells his readers to "spur one another on toward love and good deeds" (10:24), and "do not forget to do good and to share with others, for with such sacrifices God is pleased" (13:16).

James affirms that "faith by itself, if it is not accompanied by action, is dead" (2:17). Paul taught that genuine saving faith, and faith alone, justifies man before God. But it is that same faith that produces good works. Works witness to the reality of one's faith. Thus says James, not contradicting Paul, but in complementing his teaching, "You see that a person is justified by what he does and not by faith alone" (2:24).

James also makes this strong statement: "Anyone, then, who knows the good he ought to do and doesn't do it, sins" (4:17).

John, in his letters to the seven churches of Asia Minor, reminds them that the Lord knows all about their spiritual condition, especially their works. To the churches at Ephesus, Thyatira, Sardis, Philadelphia, and Laodicea, this divine reminder is given: "I know your deeds" (Rev. 2:2, 19; 3:1, 8, 15).

In the final chapter of Revelation, the tenth verse from the end of the Bible, Jesus speaks, "And, behold, I come quickly; and my reward *is* with me, to give every man according as his work shall be" (22:12, KJV).

COMPASSION FOR THE POOR

An emphasis of both Old and New Testaments is compassion for the poor. Though Jesus and his disciples carried a bag with meager financial assets, he continually taught them to care for the poor. When Mary anointed Jesus with perfume costing the equivalent of a year's wages, Judas asked, though insincerely, why the ointment wasn't sold and its proceeds given to the poor (John 12:3-6). When Judas left the last supper, some of the disciples thought their treasurer had gone to give something to the poor (John 13:29). When Jesus impacted Zacchaeus, the dishonest, rich tax-czar of Jericho, he immediately gave half his goods to the poor (Luke 19:8).

In Jesus' teaching of a coming judgment, note the reasons he gives for which the righteous will be rewarded:

"I was hungry and you gave me something to eat,

I was thirsty and you gave something to drink,
I was a stranger and you invited me in,
I needed clothes and you clothed me,
I was sick and you looked after me,
I was in prison and you came to visit me"
(Matt. 25:35-36).

Hospitals, child-care systems, schools, nursing homes, and similar institutions arose from the realization of Christian responsibility for the financially handicapped. Many institutions and centers for the sick, infirm and elderly bear the name of Luke, Peter, Barnabas, or Good Samaritan, but it's hard to find one named after an atheist or an agnostic. I haven't heard anyone say they were going to be operated on at Voltaire's Hospital.

Angola maximum security prison in Louisiana, with well over 5,000 inmates, houses the worst of the worst—murderers, kidnappers, rapists, and armed robbers. Sentences are long, often for life. Eighty-five percent will die there of disease or old age, often suffering wretched deaths alone. Burial involves digging a hole, placing the body in a cardboard coffin in the ground, then throwing dirt in the hole, often collapsing the top.

But the harsh life is softening, largely because of Christian influence. No longer do inmates have to die alone. The prison has instituted a hospice program in which prisoners take care of each other in their final days. One inmate said that he had been selfish most of his life, but that changed the first time he had to bathe a dying inmate. "When I got through bathing him and got him back in his bed, he told me, 'I appreciate that.' And it just did something to me." In caring for each other they become a thankful family. Inmates are now buried in proper coffins, made by fellow inmates. The teachings of Jesus have made an impact.

Feeding the hungry, hospitality for immigrants, shelter for the homeless, clothing for the needy, treatment for the sick, and visitation of prisoners do not exhaust the catalogue of good deeds. Rather, the list is diverse and limitless. For example, one possibility for many followers of Christ is that of taking a Sunday school class. To be a faithful and caring teacher of a group of boys or girls is a demanding but gracious and important good work.

Dr. Howard Hendricks, longtime professor at Dallas Seminary, was a Sunday school teacher in the Philadelphia area in his youth. Because a boy in his class became a serious problem, he told his superintendent, "Either the boy goes or I go." The superintendent suggested he visit the boy's home. Hendricks found a tumbledown house on the edge of town. A shabbily dressed woman, the boy's mother, answered the door. When she learned that the visitor was her son's Sunday school teacher, she invited him in. On the floor lay an intoxicated man who had been there in a stupor off and on for months—the boy's father. From then on, the teacher gave the boy more time, often taking him to major league baseball games. Some years later the boy entered Dallas Seminary. Incoming students were giving their testimony at an early fellowship. The boy rose and said, "I'm here because of my Sunday school teacher, Dr. Hendricks."

Hall of Fame TV sports commentator and former major league catcher, Joe Garagiola, put it, "When I get to Heaven, I don't think God is going to ask me for a long list of achievements, but He'll simply ask to see if my hands look rough and callused from helping people."

Eternal life is a gift from God in Jesus Christ, apart from any merit of our own.

But once we accept the gift of salvation, the reality of our faith is demonstrated by our love to our fellow human beings. God expects us to take advantage of every opportunity to be a doer of good. And if we do not become weary in the doing of good—if we stay faithful in our service—God will reward us for our life of good works.

Keep on keeping on. Who does God's work will get God's pay.

Chapter 2

The Nature of Good Works

In Somerset County, Pennsylvania, just ten miles from the site of the United Flight 93 crash on 9/11, when several heroic passengers attacked the plane's hijackers, another valiant event took place ten months later in July 2002. Nine miners were working the second shift on a Wednesday when a wall burst in an abandoned mine, sending tons of water pouring toward the men. Running for their lives from the cold, rushing torrents, the miners found a four-foot pocket in which to hide. Buried 240 feet below stone, the men huddled together, seemingly doomed to a slow, horrifying death, threatened by drowning, hypothermia, and carbon monoxide, and subsisting on little more than a corned beef sandwich split nine ways.

Unwilling to give up on these men, an army of rescue workers began boring through the sandstone to make way for a 30-inch wide rescue shaft. Despite a severe setback, they broke through to the miners just after midnight Saturday. After nearly seventy-eight hours, the first miner was pulled from the rescue shaft, and on Sunday morning at 2:44 a.m. all nine were rescued. After desperate, anxious days of watching and waiting, cheers broke out across the little towns of coal country, reverberating nationwide as the images of the miners were flashed on TV. Everyone admired the tireless efforts of those who rescued them.

Almost daily the media carries stories of people's kind acts toward their fellow-citizens, often at great personal sacrifice and in dangerous circumstances. Firemen rescue children from burning buildings. A caregiver gives unstintingly of herself in nursing a helplessly ill patient through a terminal illness. Undercover police daringly break up a drug ring. A neighbor struggles with a stranger, foiling the attempted kidnapping of a little girl. Friends comb the woods all night searching for a missing boy. A lifeguard pulls a drowning swimmer to safety. A lost wallet is returned. A helicopter makes a precarious landing on a narrow ledge to airlift several mountain climbers to safety. How do we explain such unselfish conduct? The answer is the common grace of God.

Common grace is God's kindness to all mankind short of the special grace of salvation. For example, God causes his sun to rise on the evil and the good, and sends rain on the righteous and the unrighteous. You don't have to be virtuous to soak in sunshine; the villainous enjoy it too. Rain falls on the fields of both the Mafia and the Christian. The gifts of nature flow to people commonly, both good and bad.

Also, common grace displays itself in the restraint of evil in the human condition. Our world reeks of terror, violence, and disorder, but how unimaginably awful it would be were it not for God's goodness in holding back wickedness and urging the human spirit toward order, decorum, and virtue. Apart from common grace anarchy would run amuck.

A third facet of common grace is the ability of unbelievers to perform acts of civic good. When Adam and Eve, created in the image of God, sinned by disobeying the divine command, the image of God in our first parents was scarred, and a bent toward evil passed on to every member of the human race. However, the image of God in each person was not totally destroyed, but instead was vitiated, so that aspects of that original likeness remained. Every baby born into the world since has been born with the image of God, though with a blemished likeness to be sure. Because of this image, people possess an ethical impulse and are able to perform civil righteousness and works in harmony with the laws of God.

Dr. Richard J. Mouw, president of Fuller Seminary, in his delightful book on common grace, *He Shines in All That's Fair*, proposes that God takes delight in his creation, for in Genesis 1 he repeatedly pronounced it "good." God enjoys a beautiful sunset, a well-crafted piece of literature, a work of art, good wit, athletic achievement, a symphony concert—all a part of his creation. Mouw also suggests that God is the author of acts of kindness by non-Christians that meet the criteria of righteousness and morality, but at the same time noting that morally laudable deeds do not merit salvation.[1]

Tragically, charitable deeds often give the doers a sense of false security because they believe such works will gain them favor with God. According to a *Newsweek* poll, 75% of Americans believe that their actions on earth determine whether they'll go to heaven.[2] Paul reminds us, "I know that nothing good lives in me, that is, in my sinful nature" (Rom. 7:18). We possess no goodness that can merit divine forgiveness.

So, as we hear the news day by day, we readily applaud those accounts of noble, moral and charitable behavior that occur frequently near and far, often by non-believers. But in this book the scope of good works will be confined to those who are believers. The people in Galatia whom Paul exhorted to "not become weary in doing good" were followers of Christ.

THE QUALITIES OF A GOOD WORK

(1) A prime quality of a good work is that it must proceed from a redeemed heart. The sinful human heart needs redemption. When an individual, convicted of personal sin, comes to understand that Jesus paid the price for his sins by his death on the cross, and in repentance and faith in Christ receives pardon for his sins, the realization of sins forgiven and the joy of salvation should flood his soul with thankfulness.

The heart of a person touched by God's love in Christ coming down vertically into our lives should then reach out horizontally to others around us. Paul wrote to the church at Colosse, thanking them for "your faith in Christ Jesus and of the love you have for all the saints" (1:4). A good deed is an outward act of benevolence proceeding from the internal principle of love for Jesus Christ.

To motivate ourselves to do good works, we need to ponder the cross of Jesus often. That's why the ordinance of the Lord's Supper was given us. Meditation on the sufferings and death of Jesus melts our hearts and rekindles the flame of our devotion. Paul Rees once said, "We are not so much overworked as we are under-motivated. We could go the second mile if we felt glad about it." If we are away from good works, perhaps we are away from our first love. In that case, we need to "Repent and do the things you did at first" (Rev. 2:5). To the backslidden Peter who had so easily denied the Lord three times, Jesus asked in effect, "Do you love me? If you have love for me, then show it by doing a good work. Feed my sheep" (John 21:15-17).

Love flowing from a redeemed heart will do good deeds.

(2) Good works should occur at the appropriate time and place. A better work takes priority over a good work.

Attending a church service when we should be attending a sick family member is not the better choice. Martha's work of harried preparation of a dinner for Jesus was not as good as Mary's choice of sitting at his feet to learn. The Samaritan in Luke 10 who stopped to take care of the wounded Jew is known as the "Good" Samaritan. To him, his neighbor was anyone in need, even though belonging to another ethnic group. The priest and the Levite who deliberately avoided helping the victim failed to do good, even though likely on their way to perform religious ministry functions. The Good Samaritan offered aid at a timely moment. The degrees of responsibility seem to begin with our own family (1 Tim. 5:8), then to the family of believers, then to all people (Gal. 6:10).

Jesus frequently ran into opposition from those who would religiously observe the Sabbath, even if it meant refusing to help someone who was sick. Jesus taught that healing a man with a withered hand, or doing a work of mercy, was more important than punctilious observance of the Sabbath. Jesus pronounced a woe on Pharisees who observed a rigorous tithing of minuscule garden herbs but who neglected justice and the love of God. He said, "You should have practiced the latter without leaving the former undone" (Luke 11:42).

Meeting an evident need right at our neighbor's door is a timely good work. Neglecting it is a sin. One day a lady who hadn't seen her neighbor for a couple of days knocked on her door. Looking in, she could see her neighbor sick in bed, two little children with food-smudged faces in dirty dresses playing on a messy floor, a heap of unwashed dishes in the sink, and a pile of soiled clothes near an ironing board. Waving to the sick neighbor, just before shutting the door, the visiting lady called out, "If there's anything I can do to help, please let me know."

C. W. Vanderbergh wrote:

> To love the whole world for me is no chore;
> My only real problem's my neighbor next door.

If we don't perform some works at the moment, the opportunity will be lost forever.

As a poor young lawyer in Springfield, Illinois, Abraham Lincoln was headed for his office one morning when he saw a little girl standing beside a trunk, crying at the door of her house. He stopped to see what was the matter. She sobbed out her story. She was going to visit a little friend of hers in another town. It was to be her first ride on a train, but the expressman hadn't yet come for her trunk. Lincoln lifted the trunk onto his shoulder and started off, calling to the little girl to "come along." They just caught the train. The little girl never forgot the man who was never too busy to be kind. No one can meet every need and fill every opportunity, but when an occasion for a good deed stares us in the face, we should fill it.

(3) A good deed is one performed willingly, cheerfully, and gracefully. Too often we do some kindness, threatening, "I'll do it this time but no more." Grumbling as we do some favor may disqualify it as a good work. We are told to give generously and gladly (2 Cor. 9:6-7). A gift may be marred by the ill grace with which it is given. It's not how much, but how well we give. Paul commanded that if we are showing mercy, we should do it cheerfully (Rom. 12:8).

(4) A good deed does not need a reward. We have a close friend who decorates her home most lavishly for Christmas and Easter, and invites many to see it. In addition she is a marvelous cook and serves delicious, several-course meals,

entertaining people who could never reciprocate. She sends several hundreds of cards to folks "who wouldn't get any." She makes meals and shares with others who are unable to cook. She drives people to hospitals for operations, and sits and waits till the surgery is over. As a former nurse, she can explain doctor's orders to confused relatives. She does the wash for a friend who has no machine.

Jesus said, "If you do good to those who are good to you, what credit is that to you? Even sinners do that. And if you lend to those from whom you expect repayment, what credit is that to you?.... But love your enemies, do good to them, and lend to them without expecting to get anything back. Then your reward will be great, and you will be sons of the Most High, because he is kind to the ungrateful and wicked" (Luke 6:33-35).

Jesus taught that when we throw a dinner we should invite the unlovely, maimed, lame and blind, those who cannot return the favor, rather than those who will invite us back. Many good works are subconsciously quid pro quo, something done for a possible repayment, even larger, sometime down the road. But that's not genuine helping; rather it's a sort of negotiating, bargaining, or commercial speculation. A truly good deed is uncontaminated, without ulterior motive.

(5) A good work will be rewarded. Though a person does not do a kind act primarily to get a reward, it must be noted that the expectation of reward is held up by Jesus as a legitimate reason for performing good deeds (Luke 14:14). When Peter asked what the disciples would get out of forsaking everything to follow Jesus, the Lord did not rebuke him for asking such a mercenary question, but promised dividends both in this life and in the life to come (Matt. 19:27-29). John warned against losing a full reward (2 John 8).

Though salvation is free, good deeds earn crowns. So, reward is a valid incentive for doing good deeds. As long as the love of Christ is the main compulsion (2 Cor. 5:14), the thought of reward as a secondary motive does not disqualify the act from its "good" status. Many saints through the centuries have expressed their intention to cast any rewards or crowns at the feet of Jesus in worship and adoration.

The Philippian church sent financial aid time and time again to Paul when he was in need. For example, when a prisoner at Rome, Paul had to pay the rent and food to stay in his "hired" house. Paul thanked them, "…it was good of you to share in my troubles…. Not that I am looking for a gift, but I am looking for what may be credited to your account" (4:14-17). The word "account" is a commercial term. Sharing in Paul's labors, they would share in his profits. The doing of good works is a way of laying up treasure in heaven where neither thieves, nor rust, nor a steep drop in the Dow Jones average can make a dent (Matt. 6:19-21).

Jesus declared that even the insignificant act of giving a cup of cold water to one of the least of his followers would not go unrewarded (Matt. 10:42).

(6) A good work is done unobtrusively. A seeming contradiction exists in the Sermon on the Mount. In one place Jesus says clearly, "Let your light shine before men, that they may see your good deeds and praise your Father in heaven" (Matt. 5:16). A little later, he says, "Be careful not to do your acts of righteousness before men, to be seen by them" (Matt. 6:1). Is Jesus canceling his previous instructions? Not at all. In the first instance, Jesus speaks of moral conduct, commanding us to upright lives which our fellow men cannot help but see, and when they observe these lives, they will glorify God who has

given such moral impetus to people. In the second instance, Jesus is prohibiting making a show of our kind acts, unlike the Pharisees who made a great display of their works of mercy. When we help the poor, let's make sure our motive is to glorify God and not to earn a reputation as a heavy giver or philanthropist. We don't hide our chaste life from the world, but when we do a kind act to someone, we should do it inconspicuously, not drawing attention to ourselves.

Jesus said, "Be careful not to do your acts of righteousness before men, to be seen by them…. So when you give to the needy, do not announce it with trumpets….do not let your left hand know what your right hand is doing, so that your giving may be in secret" (Matt. 6:1-4). The verb "to be seen" also gives us the word, "theater." If we give to play to the grandstand, the attention we get is our reward. There'll be none in heaven, for the work was not good. After the death of C. S. Lewis the *London Times* said he was prodigally generous with his money, but that his liberality was accompanied with such secrecy that his closest friends never fully realized its scope.

The famous Baptist preacher Charles Spurgeon and his wife refused to give away eggs their chickens laid, but would sell them. Even close relatives had to pay for them. Some branded the Spurgeons as greedy and selfish. They did not defend themselves. The full story was revealed only after Mrs. Spurgeon's death. All proceeds from the sale of eggs went for the support of two elderly widows. Because the Spurgeons were unwilling to let their left hand know what the right hand was doing, they endured the criticism in silence.

(7) A good work must be done in love. In his great love chapter (1 Cor. 13) Paul says, in effect, "I may be a great orator, but if I have not love, I'm only a clanging gong. Though I

know the Bible thoroughly, have a theological degree, understand all its mysteries, and have faith that can remove mountains, I am nothing. If I give all my wealth to feed the poor, and pay the supreme price as a martyr, I gain nothing." Service without love is profitless. It's like the Sunday school teacher who threatened her unruly, rowdy class, "I want you to understand the love of God, even if I have to beat it into you."

A man who fractured a bone in his foot had to hobble around with a cane for several days. The painful experience was eased by those who treated him kindly. People opened doors, made room in elevators, guided him across busy streets. He was tempted to keep the cane longer than he needed it. The day he left his cane home, people reverted to their old pushing, jostling selves. Then it occurred to him that everyone has some sort of broken bone somewhere, not physical bones, but emotional, psychical, spiritual ones just as frail and tender. He thought it wouldn't hurt to take time off once in a while and treat people he met during the day as if they had an injured foot.

When a brilliant young Oriental student was awarded a scholarship to a Southern Christian college, students speculated as to which of them would be capable of arguing her into Christianity. Eventually her conversion took place, not by the efforts of some brilliant campus scholar, but by an unimpressive little coed. When the new convert was asked what argument the coed had put forward to win her, the Oriental student replied, "She did not use any arguments. She built a bridge from her heart to mine, and Christ walked over it."

(8) A good work glorifies God in heaven. In aiming to obey Jesus' injunction in Matt. 5:16, the danger lurks of stopping too early in the verse, going only as far as, "let your light shine

before men, that they may see your good deeds," and omitting the all-important incentive, "and praise your Father in heaven."

A poor little girl, dressed in rags and hungry, stood staring longingly in the window of a bakery at the cookies, cakes, and loaves of bread. Came along a woman who, noticing her condition, took her into the store and bought her whatever her little heart and empty stomach desired. She then took her to a clothing store and bought her several changes of clothes. Later, looking up at the lady, the little girl asked, "Say, are you God's wife?"

On a missionary tour of Africa I drove by a prison in the city of Bukava in what was then known as Zaire. Missionaries commented that prisoners in that country received no food from the jail, and ate only as relatives or friends brought food. The missionaries had a weekly Sunday evening fellowship at which they took an offering for the express purpose of providing a regular nourishing meal for needy prisoners. When prisoners learned the source of this kindness, they were more prepared to respect the name of God and listen to the message of the missionaries.

In the *Book of Common Prayer* the collect for the 22d Sunday after Trinity ends with the request that the church be "devoutly given to serve thee in good works, to the glory of Thy Name; through Jesus Christ our Lord. Amen." We have been redeemed to glorify God. Good works honor his name.

(9) A good work makes life easier for others. A Christian training college in England had only one rule of conduct which each student received on a printed card:

NOTICE
All service ranks the same with God.

You are requested to kindly do your part in
keeping this room tidy.
If you do not, someone else will have to.

A good work brings good, sometimes material goods. When gas fumes from a faulty space heater killed seven members of a family on Chicago's northwest side, the grief-stricken mother was left with a mountain of bills. The small Baptist church that the family attended collected donations to meet her severe financial needs. Others in the neighborhood chipped in. But one man who called himself a Christian sent in an envelope containing nothing but a poorly printed tract entitled, "How to Be Saved." Perhaps he had never read, "Suppose a brother or sister is without clothes and daily food. If one of you says to him, 'Go, I wish you well; keep warm and well fed,' but does nothing about his physical needs, what good is it?" (James 2:15-16). Someone once said, "If you want to give a tract to a hungry man, wrap it in a sandwich!"

How well I remember my mother on Christmas Eve afternoon, year after year, walking (we had no car) several blocks to carry groceries and $10 gifts to some less fortunate families. Paul instructed Titus, "Our people should not have unproductive lives. They must learn to do good by helping others who have urgent needs" (Titus 3:14, NLT).

A legend tells of a person permitted to visit both heaven and hell. First, in hell, he saw a vision of a vast, endless table with people gathered around it. On the table lay every kind of food imaginable—prime ribs, caviar, ice cream cake. But all the people's arms were in splints, and no one could get the food to their mouths. Horrified by the vision, he went to heaven and saw the same sight, the vast table covered with every possible delicious food, and people whose arms were likewise in splints gathered around. The only difference was that here they were feeding each other. A good deed is one that helps another out.

Some people give indiscriminately. But with no way to check out a sob story they would rather be suckered than to miss a genuine opportunity to alleviate a need. A lady, who annually gave away unwanted but still usable family clothing, wanted to find a worthy recipient for her husband's gray overcoat with a beautiful fur collar. She recalled a self-ordained street preacher in the city's slum area who wore several layers of shirts to keep warm in frigid weather, and who collected bottles and empty cans along the river bank to make ends meet. Driving down to that area, she spotted him. Stopping her car, she called out, "Do you know of anyone that could use a winter coat?"

"Yes, yes," he enthusiastically replied. "I'm going to visit a man who needs a coat."

"Oh, yeah," the lady said to herself. "He's probably got some scheme in mind." But she gave him the coat.

Two weeks later she spotted the preacher again, collecting bottles along the riverbank. He was not wearing the coat. Angry at first, then disappointed, she glumly thought, "He probably sold it." Just then a second man emerged from the river brush with a grocery cart full of bottles and joined the preacher. The preacher's companion was smartly dressed in her husband's old coat.

Maybe some day we'll discover that many of those times when we wondered if we were being taken, we were really helping someone with a real need. And the times we were deceived we probably didn't miss the money we gave away.

SOME SUGGESTED GOOD WORKS

For years my wife, Bernice, has been in a wheelchair. Yet she is determined to do a good deed every day, even if just a note of encouragement to someone who needs a lift. She does this without fanfare, not even telling me what she does. I had to urge her to write down some different and special ways to do good.

- Go to your closet. Do you need all those clothes? Give some away. I know a person who gives away an article of clothing for every new garment purchased. Another gives away any article of clothing not worn for a year.

- Before Christmas, parents of one family have their children check out all their toys and give away any still in good condition. No junky toys are allowed as gifts.

- After purchasing and reading a new Christian book, donate it to the church library.

- One lady takes a nursing home resident out to lunch once a month.

- Many people would go to church if offered a ride. A middle-aged couple drove my 80+ parents to church every Sunday morning for a few years—till my parents were unable to go. Offer to transport children to Vacation Bible School.

- When friends are sick, send notes of support, jokes, or inspirational verses. Take in some food. Pick up items at the store and clean their bathroom, dust and vacuum.

- Phone shut-ins regularly. A nurse offered to come over once a week to bathe and wash the hair of a lady with Alzheimer's, allowing her caregiver husband to run errands.

- Give a tape player to a shut-in, and offer to pick up tapes at the library.

• A busy beautician with a sick husband visits some shut-in ladies after work to cut their hair free. One man, when he cuts his lawn, also does the lawn of his elderly neighbor.

C.S. Lewis in his essay on "Good Work and Good Works"[3] defines the latter as chiefly almsgiving or helping in the parish, and separate from one's work or vocation. Paul wrote to the Ephesians to order a thief to stop his stealing and to "work, doing something useful with his own hands, that he may have something to share with those in need" (4:28). The King James puts it, "let him labour, working with his hands the thing which is good." A believer should be engaged in work that is useful and honest, producing what is good with a high quality of workmanship whether an accountant, carpenter, teacher, musician, sculptor, executive, or civic official. Doing good work on one's job is also "good works."

In *Ruth, A Portrait,* a biography of Ruth Bell Graham, we see how this remarkable lady, wife of world-renowned evangelist Billy Graham, supported his crusades, stood alongside him at presidential inaugurations, kept their home and family intact during his many long absences, and brought spiritual guidance to many through her college Sunday school class. In fact, she helped anyone who showed up at her doorstep looking for help and hope.[4] It was said that she invited into her living room types most people wouldn't allow in their yards: delinquents from the local detention home, druggies, thieves, and the deranged, serving them pizzas, fried chicken and hamburgers, and challenging them with a Christian witness. Despite her high public profile, privately she welcomed the lonely and the misfits with special warmth.

Here are other suggested good deeds:

• Maybe you could volunteer to help Habitat for Humanity

build a house for some deprived person. Interestingly, the mission statement for Habitat says one of its purposes is to exemplify "the Gospel of Jesus Christ through loving acts."

- Participate in Samaritan's Purse shoebox Christmas project.
- Assist AIDS patients. Work in pregnancy care and abused women centers.
- Seek reconciliation with your family. Be adviser to a youth group, tutor disadvantaged children, or even adopt a child.
- A Canadian friend owned several properties, one of which was rented by an elderly widow with little means. Many, many times he quietly waved the rental payment. And wouldn't teaching English as a second language to an immigrant in one's church or community qualify as a good work? There is no end to the good works waiting for us to do.

And in doing good to others you are not only serving God faithfully, but you may find that you are helping yourself. When someone asked the distinguished psychiatrist, Dr. Karl Menninger, what he would do if he felt a nervous breakdown coming on, he purportedly answered, "I would go down the street and find someone needy and immediately seek to help him." Realizing that there are no easy answers in the cure of depression and mental illness, the act of looking outside our-selves to the needs of others can prove helpful to our own mental and spiritual health.

Have you done your good deed today?

Make it plural. Have you done your good DEEDS today?

Chapter 3

Spoiling A Good Work

Rev. George and Martha Kelsey, honored by Wheaton College as the missionary alumni couple of the year 2000, served forty outstanding years of ministry in Amman, Jordan, remaining on the field through all the Middle East turbulence of that period. A major achievement was a language school where he taught Arabic to missionaries who had been called to various Middle Eastern countries. Asked by a group of consultants on language learning why he thought such a large majority of workers leave the field after one or two terms, Kelsey offered the following observations, later summed up in a letter sent to supporters:

1. Some singles feel their last chance of getting married vanishes by staying isolated in a strange culture.
2. Many parents feel they are depriving their children of good things and opportunities that they would have back in the States.
3. Single nurses are thought by family members to be the ideal choice to take care of older parents.
4. The devastating psychological impact of lack of progress in-depth in the Arabic language after the formal study stopped. Many remain on a plateau, and the

blow to their self-esteem makes them want to bail out.

5. The lack of obvious spiritual results in the lives of others causes them to question the expenditure of time, energy and money.

6. The nagging feeling that back home one could sway crowds and build a good-sized ministry in his own language and culture.

7. The inability to reconcile the cost to their home church with requested measurable goals. How do you measure progress in a language over a month?

Kelsey acknowledged that the Lord in his sovereign plan might lead persons out of cross-cultural ministry back to their own country. But he also asked prayer for the language students to have the physical, emotional and spiritual health to stay on the job, a reminder of the exhortation in Galatians 6:9, "Let us not become weary in doing good, for at the proper time we will reap a harvest if we do not give up."

THE DANGER OF WEARINESS

Galatians 6:9 begins with two concepts: first, becoming weary; second, doing good. In this book we begin with the same two concepts, only in reverse order. In the first two chapters we dealt with the doing of good; now we turn to the danger of weariness. We have considered works before weariness for two reasons. First, this is the order in the original which literally reads, "In the doing of good let us not become weary." The biblical text puts works before weariness. Second, not only is this the order of the Greek New Testament, but also the psychological sequence—we *do*, then *tire*. Of course, some people do get weary at the mere thought of work, before doing anything.

What does it mean to become weary in well-doing? The main part of the verb "to be weary" comes from the word for "bad," and means to lose spirit, to be faint-hearted, faint, flag, lessen courage, relax zeal. Paul seems to be making a pun. The words for "good" and" bad" are spelled alike in Greek except for the middle letter. "Good" is *kalos,* and "bad" is *kakos.* Paul is saying, "In the doing of good, don't be bad." Or, "Don't behave badly while performing beautifully." Paul's style is epigrammatic. He uses a concise, cleverly worded statement, in this case a pun, to make a pointed observation. Similar language appears in his second letter to the Thessalonians (3:13), penned six or so years later. This saying likely became a maxim used by believers to encourage one another to *keep on keeping on.*

How do we do our good in a bad way? The answer—by doing our good with a disheartened attitude, with flagging zeal. Imagine it's Saturday evening. It suddenly dawns on a Sunday school teacher that tomorrow is Sunday, and he hasn't even begun preparation for teaching his class. He moans, "Oh, I've got to face those little rascals in the morning, and I haven't the faintest idea of what I'm going to say. It's so hard to teach those boys. They don't pay attention. I'd better get out the quarterly and find a few verses and a story or two. Wish I didn't have to do it." That's doing good in a bad way.

The doing of good could be extended to all departments of church life like singing in the choir, serving on boards, cooking for dinners, cleaning up, serving as treasurer, taking minutes, being a youth sponsor, VBS teacher, retreat leader, and a host of other tasks. The admonition to plod on applies in all phases of church life.

To the church at Smyrna came this word of warning, "I have not found your deeds complete in the sight of God" (Rev. 3:2). Some of their works under divine scrutiny had failed to measure up. Doing good in a weary way is one way to spoil a good work.

FACTORS CONTRIBUTING TO WEARINESSS

Paul is not telling the Galatian believers that they are not doing good works, but that they must not weary in doing them. What are some conditions that cause weariness?

(1) Physical fatigue. Galatians 6:9 contains two verbs that have to do with fainting. The major significance for both verbs is spiritual fainting or moral weakness, but in some cases they do carry the meaning of physical tiredness. The last verb in Galatians 6:9, translated "faint" in the King James, is used of the 4,000 who, before Jesus fed them, were so exhausted they were in danger of collapsing—physically.

Though the weariness Paul warns about was mainly spiritual, finding ourselves at the end of our bodily resources, overcome by fatigue, may certainly contribute to spiritual weariness and quitting. As Ruth Bell Graham points out in the June 2002 *Decision* magazine, Satan likes to make us think that our touchiness is caused by a spiritual fault when we are just plain tired. She relates how the Lord didn't lecture Elijah on his shortcomings when he was so tired he wanted to quit, but rather sent an angel with food and drink. Then Elijah just lay down to sleep some more.

(2) Going through the motions. As a frequent flier you know how it is. Just before take-off a flight attendant demonstrates what to do in case of a drop in oxygen and a mask falls in front of you. You've heard it dozens of times before, often

read in a mechanical voice. You look around, and almost no one is listening. The attendant is going through the motions.

The rules may have changed, but some years ago a friend of mine employed at the United Nations, giving me a tour, pointed to a guide and said, "No girl is allowed to be a guide for more than two years. Officials feel that the spiel she gives over and over becomes meaningless rote." I also learned that guides at a famous museum, for the same reason, were not permitted to work more than two days a week.

At a railroad station in a college town, a lady professor noticed a woman, alone in her car, slumped over the steering wheel, half-laughing and half-crying. Thinking the woman might be ill, the professor approached the open window, saying, "Are you feeling all right?" Came the reply, "For fourteen years I've driven my husband to the train station every weekday morning. This morning I forgot him."

When I told this story to my wife, she reminded me of her driving our ten-year old daughter to the next town for a music lesson. My wife always prepared her a little snack. On the way one day she reminded her daughter to eat the sandwich. No answer! My wife had put the snack in the car, but she had forgotten our daughter.

How easy to go through the motions as a Christian worker. Your job is to usher. You get there early Sunday morning, gather your pile of bulletins, check the temperature, make sure the hymnbooks are equally distributed in the pew racks, the visitors' cards are in place, and the offering plates ready. Then you show people to their places, hoping they are following you down the aisle. Smiling, shaking hands, urging newcomers to sign the guest book, giving directions to the nursery to new parents with babies—all part of the job. But after some time you find yourself just going through the motions. It's becoming a bore and a chore. You are beginning to do your good work in a bad way. Perhaps you need to refresh your memory about folks who told you that it was your genuine welcome and repeated warm greeting that helped to keep them coming.

(3) Lack of results. We teach a Sunday school class, not only for months but for years, and nothing seems to happen. We sing in the choir week after week, hand out tracts regularly, go out visiting on a church team, but nothing exciting seems to result.

A man caught a bass, placed it in a small rectangular tank in his parlor, then threw in minnows for the bass to eat. One day he put a clear partition in the middle of the tank, confining the bass to one end. When he threw the minnows in the other half, the bass made a dive for them but smacked his nose against the glass partition. Jarred back on his haunches (fins), the bass waited a while before trying again, but with less gusto than the first time. Again he was jolted back. Waiting a considerable time before another try, he made his third dive, and with less enthusiasm. Again thwarted, he waited a long while, then tried feebly. Giving up, he kept swimming around his end of the tank. An hour later the man removed the partition. But the bass never made another attempt to catch the minnows, just kept swimming around his half, despite the removal of the barrier. And the bass died of starvation.

This apocryphal item shows the need for persistence. People go out visiting from the church, knock on a door, and get it slammed in their face. After a while they make a second attempt, but with less zeal. Then a third and a fourth call, but no welcome. Then somehow God removes the barrier, making the person tender and ready for a visit. But the visitor never returns and the person dies in his unreached state.

A man gave out tracts on the same corner for ten years but with no response. So one day he decided to quit. Three months later he was walking near his old spot when he noticed a young man handing out tracts on the very same corner. Walking up to him, he asked, "How long have you been doing this?" Came the reply, "About three months ago a man handed me a tract on this corner. I took it home, read it, and through its message became a believer in Jesus Christ. I came back the next week to thank the man, but he wasn't here. I looked for him two or three other times, but I've concluded that he must have died and gone to his reward. So I decided to take his place."

I had a Sunday school teacher in my teens, not a learned man, but faithful in handing out tracts on downtown corners of my home city of Hamilton, Canada with its population of a quarter-million. On a visit to my home twenty-five years later, on a busy Friday night on a stroll down our main shopping center, my wife and I noticed a man surrounded by a crowd. Getting closer, I saw my old Sunday school teacher in the center of the crowd. Guess what he was doing? Handing out tracts to all who would accept them. The following Sunday morning, as guest teacher of the Men's Class I mentioned the incident. After the class a man came up to inform me that he had become a Christian a few months earlier through a tract given him downtown by my former teacher.

(4) *A tough situation.* "We're in a difficult location," people will say. "Most of the people in this area belong to other faiths. It's a very unproductive field. Our neighborhood is so ungrateful, and known for its hardness and lack of response."

Yet the early church flourished in the hardest of all places, the city where Jesus was rejected and crucified. Despite this disadvantage, the disciples multiplied in the city of Jerusalem, in a short time growing to a total of 5,000 (Acts 4:4). The story of the book of Acts is the account of victory after victory of the gospel in tough places until it spread all the way to Rome and reached right into Nero's elite household guard.

(5) The monotony of a task. Sometimes weariness comes through the sheer monotony of an assignment: keeping financial records for a church group, regular transporting of a boy's club, and the relentless grind of a lively, weekly youth group.

A chaplain was visiting a hospital ward of dying soldiers in England. One of the patients asked the chaplain to write his Sunday school teacher of a decade before and simply tell her that because of her teaching he would die a Christian. A few weeks later the chaplain received a letter from the teacher that said, "May God have mercy on my soul. Only last month I resigned my class because I felt that my years of teaching had done no good. Then your letter arrived telling how my teaching had influenced this boy. I have gone back to our Sunday school superintendent and asked for my class back."

I think of my own father, a stockbroker, who ushered down the same aisle in our well-attended church of my childhood for forty years. A co-usher manned his aisle for fifty years. A lady cooked the meal for the senior citizens monthly dinner for twenty years, happily dispositioned, without complaint, as unto the Lord.

A plaque on the door of our Sunday school beginners' department honors a lady who taught the four- and five-year olds for a straight 45-year period, and reads, "a lifetime of service to the Lord." Her husband, every Tuesday afternoon over a long period of time, used to visit a paraplegic unable to hold a newspaper, and read to him portions of major stories from the *New York Times.* I learned this only because I once chanced to make a visit on the paraplegic in the middle of their session. Another thing this self-effacing gentleman did every Sunday for the forty years of my pastorate was to place a pitcher of fresh water on a shelf under the pulpit. (Could I have been dry?) Only once did I ever use the pitcher. It was a spring Sunday evening service with lots of pollen in the air. When I developed an irritating cough, I suddenly remembered his faithful weekly act of service.

Galatians 6:9 doesn't mean we must keep on doing the same job. The time may come to move to a different ministry. But we must keep on keeping on with the same zeal.

WAR WEARINESS

In the closing stages of World War II a very important decision faced Harry Truman, who had just inherited the presidency. Should we use the atom bomb on Japan? Potentially, an atomic attack would incinerate tens of thousands, inflict burn injuries, and induce the horrors of radiation illness on thousands more. Both sides already knew that the U.S. would ultimately win the war. Intelligence reports indicated that, though Japan knew this, Japan also believed that by holding out months longer, issuing peace feelers, they would weaken the determination of the U.S. to fight to the bitter end. Not wanting to submit to unconditional surrender, Japan played for time, hoping to gain a better bargaining position in a negotiated peace. They counted on U.S. war weariness, or some miracle, to lead to a compromised outcome. On their part, U.S. leaders estimated that to win the war by a successful invasion of Japan would cost up to a half-million lives. To avoid such a massive loss of life, two bombs were dropped, which brought the war to a quick conclusion with total capitulation by Japan. War weariness had been pre-empted.

We're in a spiritual war. We cannot afford to let war weariness cripple our battle for doing good works. A few years ago Pastor Mathew Woodly, after eight years as senior pastor of a Long Island church, asked God for an early retirement from evangelism. The church had only a trace of spiritual growth. And he says, in *Decision* magazine (June 2002), "in me, the fire of Christ's compassion had slowly turned to icy cynicism. I was sick and tired of people. Needy people. Petty people. Dysfunctional people. They were legion, and I resented their pain and brokenness. I made God an offer, 'Here I am, Lord. Send me to Cancun.'"[5]

Instead the Lord sent him on a vacation to his wife's hometown in Montana. Sitting in a park, immersed in a novel, he saw three unkempt children plop in the grass near him. Not wishing to talk, he avoided eye contact, but before he could sneak off, the oldest child launched into a story of a tangled family. The children, 12, 10, and 6, had different fathers. One dad was dead; a second had disappeared; and the third, abusive, was being divorced by their mother who then was with her new boyfriend at the casino. The kids were to stay in the park for two hours. Then the oldest child asked, "What's your job?" In low voice he told them he was a pastor.

After a long pause, she said softly, "Pastor, we've been to church a few times and heard stories about Jesus healing and feeding people. Why doesn't he do that any more? Where is Jesus today?"

He gave them a five-minute lecture on the doctrine of the

incarnation. It was cold and detached. The three children stared back at him with love-hungry eyes. Says the pastor, "The glacier of icy cynicism in my soul melted." He started over and told them that Jesus was alive, about how much he loved them, and how nothing could separate them from his love, not abuse, homelessness, or our own sin.

He says, "I don't know if my words helped them, but I do know that God used this encounter to ignite again Christ's fire of compassion in my heart."

ing, gradual, simmering, growing, insidious, low-grade spiritual fever. As it builds up, you slow down. The reason people don't deal with it is because they do not accept it as a "form of self—self-indulgence, self-pampering, self-pity."[6] Gesswein suggested that discouraged people cry on the Lord's shoulder when they should be leaning on his everlasting arms. He insists that discouragement must be recognized as sin, dealt with and refused, with no place given it. It has been called "leukemia of the soul." D.L. Moody reputedly said, "I have never known God to use a discouraged person."

PAUL PRACTICED WHAT HE PREACHED

Our text forbidding discouragement was written by a person who practiced what he preached. If anyone ever had a right to get discouraged, it was the apostle Paul. In his second epistle to the Corinthians, Paul lets his hair down several times to list the numerous problems that could have discouraged him. He speaks of hardships, distresses, beatings, imprisonments, riots, sleepless nights, hunger (6:4-5). Later in the epistle he writes,

> Three times I was beaten with rods, once I was stoned, three times I was shipwrecked, I spent a night and a day in the open sea, I have been constantly on the move. I have been in danger from rivers, in danger from bandits, in danger from my own countrymen, in danger from Gentiles; in danger in the city, in danger in the country, in danger at sea; and in danger from false brothers. I have labored and toiled and have often gone without sleep; I have known hunger and thirst and have often gone without food; I have been cold and naked (11:25-27).

And then he adds, "Besides everything else, I face daily the pressure of my concern for all the churches" (v. 28). Imagine the strain of thirty annual church business meetings! In spite of it all he wrote, "We do not lose heart" (2 Cor. 4:1).

A fable tells of two frogs tossed into a large pail of cream. The first frog croaked immediately, "I'm done for. It's all over for me." Down he went to drown in the cream. But the second frog refused to get discouraged, muttering, "I'm not giving up without a struggle." So he kicked and kicked, churning the cream. Next thing he knew he was sitting on a layer of butter. Gesswein suggests that we could write "second frog" over 2 Corinthians. Paul lists his trials and testings, distresses and difficulties, losses and crosses. Refusing to be like the first frog, he never once mentions discouragement. Instead of becoming a croaking Christian, he was a glorying Christian. What was his attitude toward his massive and almost overwhelming trials? The Amplified Version puts it, "We do not become discouraged" (4:16).

When a cat is dropped from a height of several feet, it doesn't land on its back, but usually on its feet. You could throw Paul over the wall in a basket, or throw him into shipwreck, or throw him into jail, but he always landed on his feet and never in discouragement. When he was imprisoned at Rome, he could have moaned that he no longer could move around to proclaim the gospel. But instead of giving up, he saw it as an opportunity to advance God's kingdom. He preached and taught daily in his own hired house about the Lord Jesus. He won many to saving faith, including Philemon's runaway slave, Onesimus. He wrote many letters, four of which have made their way into the New Testament, known as the prison epistles. Some of the guards to whom he was chained became believers and carried a witness right into Nero's inner circle.

Paul has been likened to the figure "6" which, when upended, becomes a "9." When vicissitudes came his way, instead of giving up, he let the Lord use them to bring greater value out of his ministry. Notice how often the word "always" is associated with Paul: "always confident," "rejoicing always," "praying always," "always bearing about in the body the dying of the Lord Jesus," "always exercising myself to have a conscience void of offense," "giving thanks always," "always having all sufficiency in all things," "always abounding in the work of the Lord." No wonder Paul called God "the God of all comfort," who comforts and thereby encourages us in our troubles (2 Cor. 1:4).

TRY, TRY AGAIN

Harry Truman, a man of remarkable courage who refused to be discouraged, was brought up on the precept, "If at first you don't succeed, try, try again." His father would say, "Never, never give up." In the book *Truman*, by David McCullough, chapter 5, titled "Try, Try Again" begins with a quote by Harry Truman, "I've had a few setbacks in my life, but I never gave up."[7] One famous setback he freely admitted was the failure of his haberdashery.

But when it came to his political career, he had the determination to fight every step of the way, and the will to win. His most startling victory was winning the 1948 presidential election. Despite the universal predictions of a Dewey landslide, he won against the greatest odds in the annals of presidential politics. Not one polling organization had been correct in its forecast. No single radio commentator or newspaper columnist, or any of the hundreds of reporters who covered the campaign had called it right. Every expert had it wrong. Comedian Fred Allen joked, "Harry Truman was the first president to lose in a Gallup and win in a walk." The *Chicago Tribune* came out with an edition with the front-page headline gaffe, "Dewey Defeats Truman." When the final count showed his win over Dewey by two million votes, opponents granted, "We have to take off our hats to a beaten man who refuses to stay licked."

John Newton, after two rejections for ordination in the church of England, became an Anglican pastor, preaching to a congregation of 2,000 every Sunday morning and evening. He also wrote the ever popular gospel song, *Amazing Grace.*

G. Campbell Morgan was rejected as a candidate for the ministry at age twenty-five. His father wired him a telegram of encouragement, "Rejected on earth, accepted in heaven." In the next twenty-five years Morgan won worldwide acclaim as pastor, Bible expositor, author, and college president.

Many excellent books would never have seen the light of day had authors stopped submitting and re-submitting their manuscripts. The Dr. Seuss books for children have been an institution for nearly seventy years. Yet back in 1937 when an early manuscript, *And to Think I Saw It on Mulberry Street,* was submitted, the publisher replied, "It is too different from other juvenile books on the market to warrant it selling."

The Peter Principle was rejected thirteen times before published in 1969 and selling 7 million copies in thirty-five languages. Golding's *Lord of the Flies* was rejected twenty-three times, but he became the Nobel Prize winner in literature.

The Diary of Anne Frank was rejected on its first submission. The editor wrote, "The girl doesn't, it seems to me, have the special perception of feeling which would lift that book above the curiosity level."

Madeleine L'Engle's *A Wrinkle In Time* took two-and-a-half years and forty-two rejections to get a publisher. When it did come out, the publisher told her, "This book is not going to sell." Then it took off like a skyrocket.

The Tale of Peter Rabbit was turned down so many times that the author, Beatrix Potter, initially published it herself.

Susannah Wesley, mother of John Wesley, was asked by her husband why she told one of the boys to do something twenty times. "Because," she answered, "if I had only told him nineteen times, and he did it on the twentieth, all the nineteen times would have been wasted."

Chris Witty, member of the US women's speedskating team, was considered a likely medal winner in the 2002 winter Olympics. Training vigorously, she began to notice fatigue, feeling as if she were dragging an anvil along the ice. In January doctors diagnosed mononucleosis, an illness that can take up to a year for recovery. She didn't have a year; she had only four weeks before the competition. She had to cut back on her pre-Salt Lake City training to come back from the strength-sapping sickness. She said, "My energy level is day to day. It's been tough because one day I feel tired, the next day I feel great. I have to rest; it's something you hate to do."

She struggled through the last four weeks. A teammate said, "Chris is such a fighter; don't count her out." A month after the diagnosis, on a Sunday night in February, she skated a flawless race, holding together on the grueling final lap while many other top skaters faded. Not only did she cap a most improbable victory, but she shattered the world record in the women's 1,000 meter race.

William Carey, an English shoemaker, was thwarted in his attempt to interest a group of ministers to send out foreign missionaries. One minister gave this now famous retort, " When God pleases to convert the heathen, He will do it without your aid or mine." But Carey persisted, offering to go himself as a missionary to India in 1793. After nearly seven years of toil in Bengal, Carey could not claim even one Indian convert.

Moving to Serampore, near Calcutta, Carey made it the center of Baptist missionary work in India the rest of his life. By 1818, after twenty-five years, over 600 converts had been baptized, and a few thousand more were attending classes and services. Among his many accomplishments he founded a college, made three translations of the entire Bible (Bengali, Sanskrit, and Marathi), and helped in numerous translations of the New Testament and portions of Scripture into many more languages and dialects. His first wife was mentally ill. One biographer wrote that Carey often worked on his translations while an insane wife worked herself up to a state of most upsetting excitement in the next room.

Ever lose anything on your computer—a letter, chapter of a book, an entire book, and have to do it all over again? One of Carey's most devastating setbacks was the loss in a warehouse fire of his three priceless translations of the complete Bible, plus his massive polyglot dictionary, and two grammar books. Imagine the painstaking assignment of translating the whole Bible again, and writing down word for word everything from Genesis to Revelation in another dialect! Just contemplate the enormity of the task of writing down the approximate 1200 chapters in the sacred Scripture! And to have to do it three times for the three different dialects! Carey did! Most people would never have recovered, but he accepted the tragedy and began all over again with even greater zeal. Carey once said, "I can plod. I can persevere in any definite pursuit." He didn't become weary. He didn't quit. He redid the dictionary, the two grammar books and the three Bible translations.

One day a worker in a missionary organization walked into a colleague's office and plunked down a sheet of paper, declaring his resignation.

"Why are you giving your resignation to me? The president's office is just down the hall. Furthermore, when you began your service, you said the Lord Jesus Christ was calling you to tell others about Him. I think you'd better present your resignation to the One who called you. Why don't we get down on our knees here, and you tell Him what you just told me. Let Him hear that you are going to quit, that things are tough, that you get criticized a lot, and that you don't see results. Tell the Lord, for He's the One who sent you."

The resigning worker paused a moment, then said, "I hesitate to do that. I'm afraid He'll tell me to stay with the job."

His colleague thoughtfully answered, "If that's what He wants, don't you think you'd better stay?"

"Yes, I think I should," said the worker, taking new courage and resolving not to turn back, but to look straight ahead and run the race with perseverance.

Another old legend pictures the devil holding a conference with his demons to remind them that discouragement really stops believers from doing their Christian duties. Discouragement, he said, was the easiest, most effortless, yet most devastating weapon. So one little demon thought he'd like to try it out.

Landing on the shoulder of a Christian, he whispered,

"You're discouraged!"

The Christian admitted, "Yes, I guess things aren't going too well."

A second time and a third time the demon's voice said, "You're discouraged!" The Christian felt a dark cloud of gloom hanging over his head and wondered how he could ever get through the day.

Hurrying back to headquarters, the little demon gleefully reported that it worked. He said, "It worked so well! I merely suggested to the Christian that he was discouraged, and soon he really was." The little demon decided to try it again.

This time he came to a believer who really knew God's Word and the need for persevering instead of fainting. When he suggested, "You're discouraged," the Christian stood erect and replied, "Me discouraged? I should say not!"

Taken back, the demon tried again, "You're discouraged and you know it!"

The believer retorted, "Me? Never! I have an all-powerful Father. My Savior is always with me by His Holy Spirit. And I will say of the Lord that He is my refuge and my fortress: my God, in Him will I trust. Me discouraged? Not for a moment!"

Back at headquarters the little demon was asked how he made out. He reported what had happened, then moaned, "Now *I'm* discouraged!"

Triumphant Christians turn the table on the devil. Someone said that for every look we take at ourselves, we should take ten looks at God. Don't look inwardly, introspectively, but upward, worshipfully, at the One who is not the God of discouragement, but of encouragement. By seeing His greatness and goodness, by hearing him say, "Look at me;

let me handle it; let me take care of this," faith will replace discouragement.

Chapter 5

A Guaranteed Harvest

Back in the sixties, Dr. Donald C. McKaig, pastor of Simpson Memorial Church in Nyack, New York, was asked to visit an elderly man in the local hospital. Looking down at the patient's face, McKaig could see he was a troubled soul. When McKaig mentioned that his church had been named after Dr. A.B. Simpson, founder of the Christian and Missionary Alliance church, the patient replied, "When I was a boy in New York City, my mother took me to hear Dr. Simpson preach." He added that his mother had been healed through the prayers of Dr. Simpson.

"Did you ever give your heart to the Lord?" asked McKaig.

"Yes, as a young man I did. But I got away from the Lord. I've been a backslider for forty years. The Lord wouldn't have anything to do with me now." The pastor, assuring him of God's love, was able to lead the patient to renew his faith.

McKaig continued to visit the 67-year-old. When he left the hospital, McKaig felt sorry for him. The man had no job, scraped along on a small pension, dressed shabbily, drove an old car, and lived in one room at a local boarding house. But he began to attend Simpson Church regularly and made a public profession of his renewed faith.

Lonely, he would often telephone McKaig for prayer. The

busy pastor, who also taught a heavy load at Nyack College and authored a weekly Sunday school lesson in his denominational magazine, always obliged. He gave hours of counsel to this needy loner. And Mrs. McKaig invited him to the parsonage for Sunday dinner quite frequently.

One day he phoned the pastor, "I want to see you." Thinking he was again down in the dumps, McKaig invited him over. On arrival he informed the pastor, "My brother and I have made our wills, and we've arranged to leave everything to your church. Whoever dies first will leave all to the surviving brother, and when he passes away, it will all go to the church. We're doing this in memory of our mother." The man's nearest relatives were twenty-one first cousins. Then the delightful bombshell burst. "It should be close to $100,000!"

Four years later the older brother, whom McKaig never met, died in upstate New York. Days later the surviving brother passed way in Nyack Hospital. None of the twenty-one first cousins contested the will. When the estate was finally probated a year later, the church learned that it had fallen heir to $125,000. Simpson Memorial, a thriving church today, used the money to build a lovely new sanctuary. It also named a room in memory of the elderly man. Today Cahart Hall is used for board and prayer meetings.

McKaig found out firsthand the meaning of "Do not forget to entertain strangers, for by so doing some people have entertained angels without knowing it" (Heb. 13:2). He also proved the promise of Galatians 6:9 that the person who doesn't lose heart in the doing of good will reap a harvest in due time. The lesson of farming with its sowing and reaping is a frequent one in Scripture. This chapter deals with three major laws of the harvest.

Law #1

THE CERTAINTY OF THE HARVEST: WHEN WE SOW, WE WILL LATER REAP

The farmer who sows in the spring expects a harvest in the fall. He would be a fool to continue sowing if a harvest did not follow. After the Flood the Lord promised to never again destroy the earth by water, adding, "As long as the earth endures, seedtime and harvest, cold and heat, summer and winter, day and night will never cease" (Gen. 8:22). The Nile Calendar (3000 B.C.) defined the state of yearly regional flooding in Egypt with three seasons: Inundation, Planting, and Harvesting, each four months long. They expected a good harvest to follow the spring planting.

Crop failures occur in nature due to drought, flood, animals and frost, but not in the spiritual realm. We are planting spiritually all the time. We all have a field to cultivate. Our harvest is potentially enclosed in what we sow. The Scriptures repeatedly promise a reward for the faithful sowing of good. "He who goes out weeping, carrying seed to sow, will return with songs of joy, carrying sheaves with him" (Ps. 126:6).

"Cast your bread upon the waters, for after many days you will find it again" (Eccl.11:1) could be paraphrased, "Do good, and eventually sometime, somewhere, you will be repaid."

"Blessed is he who has regard for the weak; the Lord delivers him in times of trouble" (Ps. 41:1).

"A generous man will prosper; he who refreshes others will himself be refreshed" (Prov. 11:25).

"He who is kind to the poor lends to the Lord, and he will reward him for what he has done" (Prov. 19:17).

Prisoner Paul wrote, "May the Lord show mercy to the household of Onesiphorus, because he often refreshed me and was not ashamed of my chains. On the contrary, when he was in Rome, he searched hard for me until he found me. May the Lord grant that he will find mercy from the Lord on that day!" (2 Tim.1:16-18).

The reaping may not come till the world to come. Or some may come in a few years in this life, as it did for the Lutheran Church in West Linn, Oregon. Around 1980 the church sponsored Rathna Reth and twelve family members, refugees from Cambodia, providing housing, food, jobs, and many other temporal items. They became active members of the church. After three years they moved to California where Reth took a job in Silicon Valley. Twenty years later, in the fall of 2000, the current pastor of West Linn received a phone call one Saturday night informing him that Reth and several family members would be visiting the Sunday morning service. Although contacts had been rare during the seventeen intervening years, Reth, now 34, wanted to present the congregation with a check for $10,000. Across the top he had written, "In gratitude to God for everything."

When Reth stood before the congregation to make the gift, one parishioner thought he looked familiar. After the service, when Reth called him by name, the parishioner said everything clicked. He was Reth's English-as-a-second-language counselor in high school, and had helped Reth graduate on time by noticing Reth was one credit short, and by helping him sign up for a needed physical education class. Said the parishioner, "All that we did paid off. You never know when you touch a life. It's not about money. It's the fact that he's successful, thankful, and his spiritual life is in place—that's important."[8]

If we don't sow, we won't reap. If we sow little, we will reap little. Moishe Rosen, founder of Jews for Jesus, believed strongly in much sowing. His strategy was to use many types of tracts, and loads of them, including humorous, thought-provoking "broadsides," which he had his workers pass out liberally on street corners. He also took out full-page displays in national magazines and newspapers like the *New York Times*. It was his contention that widespread sowing was requisite to an extensive response to the gospel. As a result his missions saw a generous harvest.

In a *Jews for Jesus Newsletter* Rosen puts it this way: "You would not think much of a person who decides to become a farmer, buys acres upon acres of land and then goes down to the store to buy just a few seeds. Some Christians witness in the same way. Our faith does not require us to believe that every seed we plant will sprout, grow and become fruitful. What our faith requires us to do is trust that if we sow enough seed, there will be a harvest in God's field. We cannot allow ourselves to become disappointed because the first seeds we plant do not sprout and grow. Those who have witnessed over the years have encountered people who resisted the Word of God or refused to listen. Some even blistered when they understood what we were saying, but much to our surprise and joy, we later found that through other means they came to faith in Y'shua."[9]

Some day the time for sowing may be curtailed. Some day it will certainly be over. "Therefore, as we have opportunity, let us do good to all people, especially to those who belong to the family of believers" (Gal. 6:10). Dividends are guaranteed to investors in good deeds.

Whether sown in darkness, or sown in the light,

Whether sown in weakness, or sown in might,
Whether sown in meekness, or sown in wrath,
In the broadest highway, or the shadowy path,
Sure will the harvest be!"

—Author unknown

Law #2

THE QUALITY OF THE HARVEST: WHATEVER WE SOW, WE REAP THE SAME KIND

Just sowing is not enough. We must sow good seed, for whatsoever a person sows, that will he also reap. If we sow good, we will reap good. If we sow evil, we will reap evil. If we plant potatoes, we reap potatoes, not tomatoes, not turnips. We can't sow wild oats and reap whole wheat. The Bible carries vivid instances of this principle.

Jacob deceived his father Isaac in order to usurp the blessing due his brother Esau, Isaac's favorite son. And Jacob used the skin of a goat in fooling his father Isaac. Years later Jacob's sons deceived Jacob about the fate of his favorite son Joseph. And they used the blood of a goat to mislead their father Jacob.

The book of Esther, celebrated annually at the Feast of Purim, tells the story of Haman, wicked prime minister of Persia, who built gallows on which to hang the Jew, Mordecai, Esther's uncle. Providentially, through Esther's intervention, Haman ended up on those very gallows (7:9-10).

When Daniel was an administrator in the government of Darius the Mede, some associates engineered a plot that had Daniel thrown into the lions' den. The plan backfired when the animals wouldn't harm Daniel. The upshot—those administrators were tossed into the den and devoured by the lions (Daniel 6).

A child who lives with critical parents will probably learn to be judgmental. But a child reared by parents who exercise justice will likely learn fairness and evenhandedness. If we wish to reap a good kind of harvest, we had better take care to sow good seed.

Job exercised patience in the midst of terrible tragedies. Enemy attacks and storms killed his seven sons and three daughters, servants, and thousands of his livestock. Despite his extreme trials, he persisted in his faith in God. In the end God doubled the number of his livestock and made him the recipient of many gifts, blessing his end more than his beginning. The number of his children was also doubled. His first set of seven sons and three daughters were already safe in heaven. God gave him seven more sons and three more daughters, and he lived to see four generations of his offspring.

When I came to the church I pastored for forty years, my wife told me about two maiden ladies who met every Saturday evening to pray for the youth group, which was then poorly attended. They believed that a small seed of faith could remove a large mountain. Though they never lived to see it, a few decades later hundreds of young people attended the church's youth ministries. Dozens of their group went into the pastorate, became missionaries in various overseas countries, and served as directors of foreign boards or relief societies. Two of the young men ordained by our church are today senior pastors of mega churches, one in Louisiana and another in Massachusetts. Many are church leaders in areas to which they've moved.

<u>Law #3</u>

THE QUANTITY OF THE HARVEST: WE REAP
FAR MORE THAN WE SOW

We expect to reap more than we sow. Otherwise, why would the farmer plant? Crops multiply thirty, sixty, or even one hundred times. One thistledown, which blew from a boat, is said to have covered a whole South Sea island with thistles. A little acorn turns into a sturdy oak. One tiny watermelon seed goes to work in the ground, pushes up a slender vine, and builds a 40-pound watermelon.

The spies who searched out Kadesh Barnea for forty days returned with a faithless report that made the Israelites murmur, and discouraged them from going in to conquer the promised land. Their lack of faith resulted in forty years of wandering in the wilderness, one for each of the forty days of the spying expedition (Num. 14:34).

King David committed adultery with Bathsheba, then caused her husband Uriah to be killed in battle. The prophet Nathan confronted David with his adultery and murder, telling him, in effect, that because David had destroyed another man's home, David's home would be destroyed. Here's part of what happened to David's house: David's son Amnon raped his sister Tamar. Amnon was killed by David's son Absolam for violating his sister Tamar. Absolam led a revolt against his father King David, then lay "with his father's concubines in the sight of all Israel" (2 Sam. 16:22). David's army commander Joab then killed Absolam. Earlier the baby of David and Bathsheba died. Partial scorecard from David's affair with Bathsheba—three of David's sons dead and a series of rebellions, bloodshed, and violence.

Conversely, the sowing of a small good may reap a large

recompense. "Give, and it will be given you. A good measure, pressed down, shaken together and running over, will be poured into your lap" (Luke 6:38).

Malachi wrote, "Bring the whole tithe into the store-house...and see if I will not throw open the flood gates of heaven and pour out so much blessing that you will not have room enough for it" (3:10).

Jesus encouraged his followers to endure ridicule for doing good for his sake. "Blessed are you when people insult you, persecute you and falsely say all kinds of evil against you because of me. Rejoice and be glad, because great is your reward in heaven" (Matt. 5:11-12).

In the Parable of the Talents, Jesus announced this compensation for the two loyal servants who had put their talents to gainful use: "Well done, good and faithful servant! You have been faithful with a few things; I will put you in charge of many things. Come and share your master's happiness!" (Matt. 25:21-23).

One day Peter bluntly said to Jesus, "We have left everything to follow you! What then will there be for us?" Jesus replied, "Everyone who has left houses or brothers or sisters or father or mother or children or fields for my sake will receive a hundred times as much and will inherit eternal life" (Matt.19:27-29). Note the *good measure* running over, *much blessing*, the *great reward*, the responsibility for *many things, a hundred times as much*.

Chuck Colson, presidential aid and hatchet-man in Nixon's administration, was sent to prison for his part in Watergate. Becoming a Christian and burdened for the needs of people in jail, on his release Colson started Prison Fellowship Ministries with branches today in many countries.

One phase of the work, Angel Tree kids, provides for Christmas presents for children of fathers and mothers in jail who otherwise would be forgotten at Yuletide. In 2001 over 600,000 kids received gifts from the Angel Tree, including literature especially for children.

In May 2002 Colson was a speaker at the Leadership Forum in the state capitol in Florida. Taking questions after his speech, Colson was surprised when a man stood up and asked, "Would you mind very much being hugged by an ex-offender?" Thunderous applause from everywhere in the room greeted the ex-offender as he came forward, hugged Colson, and said, "Thank you so much. I came to Christ in prison because of Prison Fellowship. Now my life is back together and I'm working to make a difference in Florida."

Colson commented, "Something like this happens everywhere I go—and every time it thrills me! These are the living monuments of this ministry, the men and women whose lives have been utterly transformed by the Gospel!" Already the harvest has yielded thousands of such changed lives. And eternity will doubtless reveal thousands more.[10]

One hot summer day way back in the 1880's a young medical student was going from house to house in a farming area of Maryland, selling books to earn money for college. Near the end of the day, hot and thirsty, he called at a farmhouse where no one was home except a cheerful teenage girl who said, "Mother is a widow. We have no money to buy books." Then the student asked for a glass of cold milk instead. The thirsty student drank two glasses of milk. She would take no pay, objecting, "Mother told me to be kind to strangers."

Years elapsed. One day, as head of the hospital, the one-time medical student, now its chief surgeon, was visiting the wards when his eye fell on a face which he well recalled as the one who had given him the cold milk on that hot summer day long ago. The patient was too sick to recognize anyone. Things began to happen. She was moved into a private room with nurses around the clock. Everything known to medical science was done for her. The chief surgeon took special interest in her case.

After weeks of medical attention the patient recovered and was sitting up in her room when the nurse said, "You are going home tomorrow." The patient responded, "I'm so glad." But then with her face clouding up, said, "The cost of all this worries me—the bill must be very high." The nurse offered to go and get the bill.

As the patient looked over the items and read the staggering cost of both operation and hospital care, tears came to her eyes. "How will I ever get it paid?" she exclaimed. But when she read a little further down, her eyes caught sight of eight words which dried her tears, "Paid in full by a glass of milk." Then she read the signature, "Howard A. Kelly, M.D." The former book salesman medical student and the already renowned surgeon were one and the same.

Keep on keeping on. Who does God's work will get God's pay.

Chapter 6

Harvest Delayed

A youth adviser, retiring after several years of noble service in a church's high school youth group, received this letter from a girl who had moved away from the area a year before:

"I learned last week that you are retiring from active duty as a youth adviser. Of course, I know you deserve a nice long rest but I also know you will be missed. Maybe sometimes you look at all those gas and car repair bills, those late nights and wonder if it was really worth it. Well, let me just assure you that it was much more than just 'worth it' for us.

"You told us many times that high school years are among the most important of our life, deciding important questions such as our vocations, choice of a mate, and what standards we shall set for ourselves. I know that to make these decisions a young person must come to a realization of and love for Christ. The youth group has certainly helped many young people, myself included, to come to such knowledge. You, and the other wonderful advisers have strengthened a very real faith in me. It's the kind of faith that will carry us through everything from a chemistry exam to the loss of a husband or wife, and it's something we can share with other people and teach our children.

"I guess I rambled on a little, but just wanted to put into words some of the gratitude I have for all you've done."

The advisor who received this letter commented, "I never wrote her after she left, nor had I heard from her before. This letter came as a total surprise out of a clear, blue sky. I never felt I had gotten through to this girl."

When we sow good deeds, they will later return to us in like kind, multiplied, and in accordance with another principle of the harvest, namely that the reaping comes at a different season from the sowing. Though "he who sows righteousness reaps a sure reward" (Prov. 11:18), the harvest may be delayed. We see this in the farmer who "waits for the land to yield its valuable crop and how patient he is for the autumn and spring rains" (James 5:7). A farmer never expects a harvest the same day he sows. Nor does he rise the next morning looking for fields of waving grain. Nor does he anticipate the sight of crops within a week or a month. Rather, he waits, knowing that the harvest will come in its appointed time. The sheaf became an early Christian symbol, conveying the thought that without fail a spiritual harvest would some day be gathered in as a result of the faithful sowing of the Word.

But herein is a difference between a physical harvest and spiritual reaping. Some crops in the natural world, if sown in the fall, will yield in the spring. Or if sown in the spring, will yield in the fall. A definite time period exists between sowing and reaping. The farmer can count on the harvest appearing in a specific number of months. And with reasonable accuracy he can circle his calendar the week his crops should be ready.

But spiritual reaping does not come with any degree of temporal predictability. Spiritual results may come a few days after sowing, or a few months after, or a few decades after. We may even have to wait till we reach heaven to discover that our efforts on earth were not in vain. Reaping will take place "at the proper time" (Gal. 6:9), also translated, "in due season," "at the right time," "at the opportune season," "after a while," "in its own time." The time of joyous reaping may seem like a long time in coming, and not exactly as and when we may have wished, but it will come in God's perfect timing.

A teacher, commenting that success is not always obvious, pointed to the Chinese bamboo tree which seems to do absolutely nothing for its first four years, but which suddenly, sometime during the fifth year, shoots up ninety feet in sixty days. The teacher asked, "Would you say that bamboo tree grew in sixty days, or five years?" He likens our lives to the Chinese bamboo. Sometimes we put forth effort over and over, and nothing seems to happen. But if we do the right things long enough, we'll receive the reward of our efforts.

REAPING SOON

In church for the first time, a little boy was given a coin by his mother and coached about the offering. When the plate was passed, he deposited the coin, then asked his mother, "What will come out of the plate—bubble gum or a licorice stick?"

Our society is geared to expect early, if not immediate results from our efforts. And many times the reaping of our good deeds does come soon, as in the case of the youth advisor mentioned earlier.

Parents at graduations often see rewards for their hard years of constant training and painstaking discipline now revealed in the academic, athletic, musical, and social accomplishments of their offspring.

Sunday school teachers often take great delight in the salvation and spiritual progress of their students. I recall a problem young man in a church. He had been suspended from high school more than once. His wonderful parents were at a loss and prayed hard. His Sunday school teacher also kept caring and praying, even though his pupil kept making trouble.

Late one August the boy's peers persuaded him to attend the teenage week at a nearby Bible camp. On the Sunday night after the camp and just before Labor Day, the pastor turned a major part of the evening service over to the youth group for a report on the week at camp. The young people were so full of camp blessings that the pastor had no time for his sermon. Some had been converted. Others dedicated their lives. But the testimony that rang out loudest was the decision of this troubled boy to come to the Lord and live for him. And this he did, demonstrating the reality of his vow until as an upperclassman in a Christian college, preparing for fulltime Christian service, a physical seizure took his life.

But at the end of that Labor Day eve Sunday evening service, as people stood in the hallway, so thankful for the testimonies of their youth, a man's voice could be heard momentarily above the din. It was his high-school Sunday school teacher who had been so patient with the boy, and who had prayed for him every day. These were his words—with a big smile, "It was worth it all." That night the teacher had begun to see the first fruits of his faithful sowing, and, of course, not only his, but also of the many others who shared in the plantings.

REAPING AFTER MANY YEARS

In 1984 during his pastorate at the Christian Tabernacle in Dayton, Ohio, Wayne W. Boyer decided to attend his twenty-fifth high school class reunion. "Some had put on weight," he reported. "Others had lost hair. Some of their stories were tear-jerkers." But schoolmate Kenny brought other news. At meal-time, when Pastor Boyer was seated at the head table because he was to offer the invocation, Kenny jumped out of the food line and fairly raced over to Boyer's table. With a twinkle in his eye he exclaimed, "Hey, Wayne. I got saved!" Twenty-five years ago they had been good school friends. Now they were brothers in Christ. After a warm conversation, as Kenny turned to rejoin the line, he shouted back over his shoulder, "See, Wayne, all your witnessing to me wasn't for nothing!"

Back in the era before pensions were prevalent, a lady who all of her life had given a tenth of her salary to the Lord's work knew she would soon lose her job because of her age. Without a pension or visible means of support, she wondered what would happen to her. She always attended prayer meeting at the Baptist Temple in Philadelphia whose pastor, Dr. Russell Conwell, was also the founder of Temple University. One Wednesday evening her pastor asked for testimonies of those who had tithed for several years. Six gave glowing witness to blessings received. The seventh to speak, this frail woman of seventy, reluctantly said, "I wish I could give such a testimony, but I cannot. I have skimped and saved and denied myself through the years to keep a vow made decades ago that I would tithe my income. But now I am old, and about to have no job, and will have no income. I don't know what I shall do." When she sat down, the prayer meeting was closed in a depressing chill.

The next day Dr. Conwell was lunching with John Wanamaker, founder of the Wanamaker Department Store in downtown Philadelphia. Wanamaker said, "Dr. Conwell, I think you will be interested to know that our store is about to inaugurate a pension system for our employees. We have thought about it for years. Finally the plan has been worked out. We are about to issue our first life pension today to a woman who has served our firm for twenty-five years." Then he mentioned the name of the woman. To Conwell's amazement, it was the lady who had given the pessimistic testimony in prayer meeting the night before.

In 1987 Jack and Adelaide McDaniel were finishing up forty years of missionary service in Japan. After preaching a farewell sermon in a church he helped to start, McDaniel was approached by a fine-looking visitor, a businessman, who showed him pictures of McDaniel preaching to a group of university students back in the early 50s. He pointed to himself and commented that he had been converted at that service over thirty years earlier. He was now serving the Lord at a sister church. What pleasant news!

In many cases the years of our earthly sojourn will go by, and we'll have to wait till heaven before the Lord of the harvest reveals to us how our consistent good works, all unknown to us, played a part in drawing someone, perhaps many others, closer to him.

SEEING THE WHOLE PICTURE
When results of our good deeds are missing or minimal,

there's a tendency toward quitting. Our discouragement is exacerbated by our inability to see the whole picture. We fail to sense how God moves in mysterious ways at various times at various places and over zigzag paths to bring his harvest to fruition. In every local church, loyal workers have labored before the current generation came along to enjoy the benefits of the old-timers' sowing. In many places around the world faithful pastors, missionaries, and national workers have devotedly sown the seed, and then along came another generation to garner the results. Many evangelists in their crusades reap a harvest of souls for whom the seeds of salvation were sown earlier by godly pastors and other faithful witnesses.

But in God's great blueprint every one of his servants who has had a pivotal part in the divine scheme will reap his own reward according to his own labor for the Lord.

This concept of co-laborers sharing in the rewards of the harvest comes across in Paul's writings to the Corinthians. Divisions were caused in the church at Corinth when members began lining up behind human leaders, namely Apollos and Paul. Paul wrote, "What, after all, is Apollos? And what is Paul? Only servants, through whom you came to believe—as the Lord has assigned to each his task. I planted the seed, Apollos watered it, but God made it grow. So neither he who plants nor he who waters is anything, but only God who makes things grow. The man who plants and the man who waters have one purpose, and each will be rewarded according to his own labor. For we are God's fellow workers" (1 Cor. 3:5-9).

This harvest principle is also explained in the Gospel of John by the Lord of the harvest himself. After Jesus revealed himself to the woman at the well as the Messiah and Water of Life, she witnessed to the townspeople of Sychar. Many became believers. As the disciples gazed at the interested Samaritans, Jesus said,

> "Do you not say, 'Four months more and then the harvest?' I tell you, open your eyes and look at the fields! They are ripe for harvest. Even now the reaper draws his wages, even now he harvests the crop for eternal life, so that the sower and the reaper may be glad together. Thus the saying 'One sows and another reaps' is true. I sent you to reap what you have not worked for. Others have done the hard work, and you have reaped the benefits of their labor" (4:35-38).

Jesus told the disciples they were reaping where they had not bestowed any labor, neither sowing nor watering. But they were entering into the labors of earlier workers by bringing in a harvest of believing Samaritans.

The concept is this: Let's do what we can while and as we have opportunity, and leave the outcome to God. Some may do the job of sowing, others of watering, and still others have the satisfying task of reaping, mainly because others have done their job of sowing and watering. The one who has the exciting privilege of harvesting may not have done much labor at all, and may receive less of a prize than those who sowed and watered. "Because you know that the Lord will reward everyone for whatever good he does" (Eph. 6:8), therefore we should do all the good we can, especially since we don't know how much more opportunity we shall have.

John Wesley's *Journal* (June 1742) carries this entry, "At six I preached for the last time in Epworth churchyard (being to leave the town the next morning), to a vast multitude gathered together from all parts, on the beginning of our Lord's Sermon on the Mount. I continued among them for near three hours, and yet we scarce knew how to part. O let none think his labor of love is lost because the fruit does not immediately appear! Near forty years did my father labour here; but he saw little fruit of all his labour. I took some pains among this people too; and my strength also seemed spent in vain; but now the fruit appeared."

In the good work of prayer a harvest of answers may continue for decades. *Focus on the Family News* (July 2002) displays the photo of Dr. James Dobson's maternal great-grandfather with the notation that this ancestor "prayed from 11 a.m. to 12 noon every day for four generations of his family, both those living and those not yet born." The harvest is still being reaped in this powerful family ministry.

A lady went as a missionary to Ecuador and worked with a tribe of Quincha Indians for over a half century. During these decades she reduced their language to writing, taught the people to read and write, and started to translate the Bible into their language. However, after more than fifty years of diligent labor, she was able to count less than a handful of people who had become Christians. She retired. After spending all her working years in seemingly fruitless endeavors, she was replaced by a young couple who picked up where she had left off. Amazingly, in the next fifteen years practically the entire tribe of 15,000 Indians professed faith in Christ and joined local churches.

The first lady's half-century of missionary ministry was not in vain. Regarding evangelism both she and the couple that followed her were equally faithful. Though the first one sowed and the later couple reaped, both evangelized. Without those years of faithful and effective sowing and watering, effective reaping would not have occurred.

Believing that evangelism is a process rather than an event, Dr. James F. Engel and Dr. H. Wilbert Norton constructed a hypothetical scale of steps in evangelism, as people move closer and closer to Christ, called *The Spiritual-Decision Process.*[11] The chart begins with a minus 8 and proceeds to a plus 5. Those with a minus on the scale are pre-evangelism activities. A decision to accept Christ moves from minus 1 to zero on the chart. Those steps after the conversion experience have a plus before their numbers that mark growth in grace and progress along the Christian path.

When the first missionary went to Ecuador, the Quincha Indians were probably a minus 8, primitively aware of a Supreme Being but without any awareness of the gospel. It took years of her ministry to raise their level of God-consciousness and give them an understanding of the gospel. Every advance was a vital element in their evangelization, leading them to the place of conviction of sin and into active faith, and subsequent rich reaping under the later couple's endeavors.

The Spiritual-Decision Process chart emphasizes the need to divest our minds of the concept that evangelism takes place solely when a person makes that final step of commitment to Christ, moving from minus 1 to zero. Though the new birth may occur at a precise moment, every word, every deed, every influence of others along the way that helps move a person from minus 8 to minus 7, from minus 7 to minus 6, and so on, each and every one contributes to the moment of decision. These minus steps are usually termed pre-evangelism, but any step that brings a person closer to accepting Christ is a vital ingredient in the scheme of evangelism.

We often forget or don't realize that it usually takes the efforts of more than one person to lead an individual to Christ. On a questionnaire asking which person had led them to Christ, most respondents listed several: parents, Sunday school teacher, pastor, neighbor, fellow employee, spouse, friend. The chain leading to salvation often has many links. On one occasion, didn't it take four people to carry a paralyzed man to Jesus for healing?

Moishe Rosen points out that though it's human nature to want to be the principal agent in another's conversion, God usually uses many people to make impressions in the witnessing opportunities he appoints to win an individual. He says, "God is constantly reaching out through the Holy Spirit, wooing people, making small impressions, creating questions in people's minds and hearts. Sometimes an impression is made by a funeral oration, or the verse on a Christmas card, or classical music such as Handel's *Messiah*. These impressions are gospel seeds, the person's heart is a field, and though that heart might be hardened, all of us have seen granite cracked by the seed of a tree that lodged itself in a crevice. Thus, we can understand the proper prayer for the witnessing Christian is this: 'Lord, may you send more seed to fall on the heart of my friend, may they take many impressions of you. Open their hearts and their minds that the gospel seed which you are sowing through so many of your servants might take root.' Also, the person who would take satisfaction in witnessing must witness to many."[12]

SOME DELAYED PASTORAL HARVESTINGS

Through the years of my 40-year pastorate at Grace

Baptist Church in Nanuet, New York (1949-89), various people from time to time have made me aware that my ministry to them has proven fruitful. Well do I remember in 1961 receiving a two-paged, single-spaced letter, twelve years into my New York pastorate, from a young man in my first church back in Pennsylvania. I had lost touch with him, and his letter came as a complete surprise. He wondered if I would remember him, claiming he had been a senior high delinquent and had tested the patience of both my wife and myself with his many questions.

He had felt a call to the ministry but pursued a successful career in education, becoming an elementary principal and supervisor in eight years. Though happily married with three children, and active in many churches in many capacities, something was missing. In 1960 he offered himself for the ministry. In rapid sequence he was approved for a License to preach in the Methodist church, became a supply preacher in a Philadelphia church, and enrolled in Eastern Baptist Seminary. He ended, "I think back many times to the influence you had on my spiritual life. At the time you probably thought that love's labors had been lost. However, as you can see, sometimes it takes a while for results to be seen." The last time I heard from him he was both church pastor and school principal.

In 1983 I received a letter from someone whose name I did not recognize. He wrote, "By the way, our paths have crossed just once. Back in 1949 (thirty-four years previous) when I was a teenager living in New Hampshire, I attended LeTourneau Christian Camp at Canandaigua, New York, where you were a speaker. That was a significant couple of weeks for me. I followed the Lord in baptism and dedicated my life to Christian service at a Friday night meeting in the tabernacle. Perhaps this is a good spot to thank you for playing a part in my spiritual growth at a time I was making those decisions." He also mentioned the names of four other speakers at the camp, two of them later becoming his seminary professors, all of them making an impact on his life.

Also in 1983, after conducting a funeral for a family connected with Camp Hope, a summer ministry of Children's Bible Fellowship located fifty miles north of New York City, a young adult approached me, "Did you ever write an article back in the sixties in *Christian Life* magazine on Camp Hope?"

I assured him I did, easily recalling how deeply moved I had been by my visit to this camp to research material for the story. Severely handicapped (both physically and mentally) children enjoyed the fun of living in cabins, eating in the dining room, swimming, playing games, and listening to Bible lessons. The loving care of the young staff who had to dress, feed, often change, push these campers around the bumpy grounds, and help them into the pool impressed me. I could never forget the handicapped's vibrant, sometimes off-key singing of choruses, mouths drooling with saliva. I tried to capture this atmosphere in the article. Usually I received little response to my articles but this one probably received as much attention as any of my pieces during the years. And now this was sixteen years after its publication.

When I told the young adult that I was the author, he replied, "When I read that article back in Kansas, I could not rest till I made a trip to see that camp. I got a job as camp counselor and I have never left. I am still there after sixteen years." Later, he became the director of Hopetown, an all-year round home for handicapped young adults in the same complex, and enrolled in seminary.

It was my privilege to teach journalism at Nyack College for over a decade. One day I ran into a former student who had spent some time as a missionary in Africa. He was on home assignment, earning a graduate degree in journalism from Syracuse University. He told me that the Nyack journalism class years before had given him the impetus to pursue this area. He used his writing talent in the public relations department of his denomination, and wrote the official, comprehensive history of its missionary history, *To All Peoples: Missions World Book of The Christian and Missionary Alliance.* Robert L. Niklaus autographed his gift copy to me with these words, "Had it not been for your journalism class there may not have been such a book as this. How's that for positive writing. Gratefully."

Our church sponsored a weekly Sunday morning radio program for twenty-four years. Many letters came in, and many people visited the church as a result. One interesting episode occurred after a Sunday morning service in the mid eighties. A young man waited till most of the people had greeted me at the door. Then he approached me. "You don't know me, but I would know your voice anywhere. I am the announcer on your radio program. For the last four years I have introduced your 'Focus' show. At first I did not listen to what you said. In fact, I did not like it. But I kept hearing snatches of it, and eventually it got to me. And now I wouldn't miss it. Moreover, I have become a believer in Christ because of your program and my contact with another minister." Later he told this story in our pulpit during a regular Sunday morning service.

FAILURE MAY BE A PRELUDE TO SUCCESS

What seems like rejection may sometimes be a step toward reception. During a house-to-house canvass in a new development, a church visitor asked a homeowner a series of friendly questions, but when he got to the matter of beliefs, the homeowner became agitated, even angry, claiming that one's religious views were a private matter. The visitor was turned away, discouraged, but left some evangelical literature. Months later the new homeowner showed up at church, and later became a Christian. In giving his testimony before joining the church the new convert told of his initial negative response to the visitor's questions. But he added that when his initial irritation subsided, he decided that perhaps he should look the material over instead of overlooking it. The booklet made sense and ultimately led to his conversion.

A Campus Crusade leader received this written testimony. "Someone came to my door talking about a survey and about God, so I slammed the door in his face. But I got to thinking maybe I needed God to help solve my problems. I turned on the TV and some fellow was talking about God. I opened a book and there was something about God. So I thought I had better see if God could solve my problem, and he did."

T.J. Bach, a college student, crossing a street in the middle of Copenhagen, Denmark, in the early years of the twentieth century, noticed a young stranger deliberately cross from the other side and thrust a tract into his hand. Bach tore the tract to pieces as he told the stranger to mind his own business. The young stranger, devout in his ministry of tract distribution, thought this contact was a complete loss, and turned into a doorway to weep. When Bach saw the tears, he felt sad. He reasoned, "He's given of his time to distribute this tract; he's given of his money to buy it; and now he's giving of his love in tears." When Bach returned to his room, he reassembled the pieces of the tract, read the message, accepted Christ, and that evening publicly confessed his faith in a nearby church. Bach became a pioneer worker in TEAM, today's well-known Evangelical Alliance missionary society.

George Muller, remembered for his orphanages which he operated purely by faith and prayer, asking no man or woman for financial help, followed a similar policy in his preaching ministry. Believing that God's Word never returned void, he simply trusted the Lord to give power to the faint, and strength to the weak. In an interview late in life he said, "Sixty-two years ago I preached a poor, dry, barren sermon, with no comfort to myself, and, as I imagined, with no comfort to others. But a long time afterwards I heard of nineteen distinct cases of blessing that had come through that sermon."

Sometimes when we try so hard to do good, we become discouraged and disheartened because we think our efforts are a failure. A pastor tells of a girl who was converted in his church. One Sunday evening after church, she visited in his office and lamented, "It doesn't work. I'm just as bad-tempered as ever. No matter how much I try to do good around the home. I'm giving it up." The pastor encouraged her not to quit.

She hadn't been gone ten minutes when her father, who did not know his daughter had been in church that evening, walked into the pastor's office and plunked down on his desk a generous donation for the pastor's work among the poor of the parish. "What's this for?" the pastor asked.

"I'm giving you that," the father replied, "because since my daughter started coming here, she's not only a different girl, but our home's a different place. She's so helpful to every-body."

May not such disclosures be a miniature foretaste of reve-lations we shall receive in heaven? The Lord will unroll the canvas and show us how people whom we thought we had failed to reach, or whom we had forgotten, did have their lives altered—perhaps mildly or even radically, through our faith-ful influence.

During testimony time in a London, England rescue mis-sion's regular nightly service a sailor rose to tell his story. On a voyage to Australia, while on leave in the port of Sydney, mingling with the crowd along the wharf near midnight, this sailor saw the form of an older man emerge from the milling throng, head directly for him, and without any introduction abruptly ask, "Young man, if you were to die tonight, where would you spend eternity?" The sailor said those words haunted him, set him thinking, and led him later to accept Jesus as his Savior.

Six months later a different sailor visiting the same London rescue mission's nightly service stood at testimony time and told basically the same story. Late at night, while he was pushing his way through a crowd in the port of Sydney, Australia, suddenly the form of an older man appeared, head-ed his way, and solemnly asked, "Young man, if you were to die tonight, where would you spend eternity?" Again, this ques-tion prompted the sailor to accept Jesus as his Savior.

When the superintendent of that London rescue mission learned that the next annual meeting of international rescue mission directors was scheduled for Sydney, he determined that while there he would try to contact this mysterious figure that seemed to materialize out of nowhere to confront sailors with the gospel. So, night after night, after the evening meeting, he would join the crowds walking the harbor sidewalks, alert, eyes searching among the people, expectantly, for that elusive stranger. But without success. It came to the last night. It was late. The superintendent from London was about to give up. He had searched longer than usual.

Then it happened. Seemingly out of nowhere emerged an old man heading straight for him, then out came the probing question, "If you were to die tonight, where would you spend eternity?" Excitedly the superintendent told him about the two sailors and the testimony they had given in his London rescue mission. The old man listened intently, then quietly said, "For fifty years I have been asking sailors here in Sydney Harbor the same question, and this is the first time I have learned of anyone affected by my ministry."

Keep on keeping on. Who does God's work will get God's pay.

Chapter 7

Perseverance—Finishing God's Work

Dr. V.R. Edman, when president of Wheaton College, received the following letter from a recent graduate and shared it with the student body at a chapel service:

"Dear Dr. Edman:

"Currently I am a resident in neurosurgery. Last week it was my unusual privilege to assist in an operation on a college mate. Midway in the procedure the patient had a cardiac arrest, but because of the alertness of the anesthesiologist we were immediately aware of it and instituted heart massage without delay. Despite the massage and electrical defibrillation the heart would not pick up its own rhythm and we continued with deteriorating hopes. After the better part of an hour, as I was taking my turn at the massage, one of the team said, 'We might as well quit'—and hardly had he mouthed it than I retorted with your old chapel aphorism, 'It is always too soon to quit'—and to myself added your benediction, 'now shall we pray.' At this point the electrocardiogram spontaneously reverted to a normal rhythm, and pulse and blood pressure were bounding. We continued with the operation, and now, five days later, this patient is about to be discharged. You might pass this on to the chapel, but for professional reasons it has to be incognito."

Only eternity will reveal how many former Wheaton College graduates, reaching a very difficult spot in their careers and close to giving up, have heard echoing in their hearts Edman's unforgettable words, "It is always too soon to quit," and found them heartening and true.

How easy to become discouraged and relax our zeal in the Lord's work. How many who see no results, are at wit's end, feel cornered, and think themselves useless and forgotten. In *Lectures to My Students,* Spurgeon wrote to his ministerial candidates, "Fits of depression come over most of us. The strong are not always vigorous, the wise not always ready, the brave not always courageous, and the joyous not always happy. There may be here and there men of iron, to whom wear and tear work no perceptible detriment, but surely the rust frets even these; and as for ordinary men, the Lord knows, and makes them to know, that they are but dust."

> Oh, it is hard to work for God,
> To rise and take his part
> Upon this battlefield of earth,
> And not sometimes lose heart!
> —An unknown poet

Someone said, "Christians grow discouraged much more quickly than salesmen." Too many quit too soon. An unknown humorist describes many of us in his revision of a Longfellow poem:

Toiling—rejoicing—sorrowing,
So I my life conduct;
Each morning sees some task begun.
Each evening sees it chucked.[13]

Often the enemy is not hostility from outside, but sheer weariness from within. Hence Paul's frequent, vigorous exhortations to keep on, to endure, to be steadfast, to continue to the end: "… stand firm. Let nothing move you. Always give yourselves fully to the work of the Lord, because you know that your labor in the Lord is not in vain" (1 Cor. 15:58).

Paul urged Timothy to set an example for believers, and to devote himself to preaching and teaching. "Be diligent in these matters; give yourself wholly to them, so that everyone may see your progress. Watch your life and doctrine closely. Persevere in them, because if you do, you will save both yourself and your hearers" (1 Tim. 4:15-16). Though directed at a younger pastor, these words are applicable to all believers.

The book of Hebrews was written to encourage those who had made a profession of faith in Christ to keep on with Christ. Don't go back to Judaism but go on with Jesus who is superior to angels, Moses, and the Aaronic priesthood and sacrifices. "Let us hold unswervingly to the hope we profess, for he who promised is faithful" (Heb. 10:23).

Reformed theology holds strongly to the doctrine of the perseverance of the saints. This perseverance refers not only to salvation but to service as well.

AMAZING STORIES OF PERSEVERANCE

Examples abound in secular life of those with poor starts or imposing setbacks who have persisted and overcome, hanging in there—not just hanging. Visiting an inmate in a federal detention in lower Manhattan, I noticed on the wall of the office where we were permitted to talk, a framed plaque that listed over a dozen setbacks in the first fifty years of Abraham Lincoln's life. Hoping that familiarity with Lincoln's experience might be some sort of an inspiration to the young inmate, I asked him to copy and mail me these facts, which he did. They included Lincoln's two failures in business, the death of his sweetheart, his nervous breakdown, two defeats to become a member of Congress, two defeats to become a senator, and his defeat for the vice-presidency of the United States. That's the record of a man who would not give up despite repeated losses, but who persevered until at fifty-one he was elected president.

William and Mary College in Virginia was damaged and closed during the Civil War. After a precarious opening, the college again went into a period of suspension which lasted seven years. But every morning during those seven barren years the president rang the chapel bell. Though without students and faculty, the president still rang the bell, believing that intellectual life would again fill those halls—and it did!

A teenager seemed destined for failure. He ranked third from the bottom in his class. Comments by his teachers included, "He is certainly no scholar and has repeated his grade twice. He seems to have little or no understanding of his schoolwork. At times he seems almost perverse in his ability to learn. He has not made the most of his opportunities." Yet he became one of the greatest statesman the world has ever known—Sir Winston Churchill.

A boy had no particular interest in music except for a short time in junior high school when he joined the glee club and took part in their first concert. The next morning the teacher said, "Somebody ruined the concert last night and I'm going to find out who." She made each singer sing several little phrases individually. When she got to this boy, she made him sing again and again, and then said, "You're the one, out you go!"

The boy, ashamed and discouraged, said, "I was cast out in defeat." A few years later, at his first singing lesson at sixteen, his teacher was impressed with his unusual operatic voice. At eighteen he made his debut as a soloist in the San Francisco Opera Company. In 1946 he won the Metropolitan Opera's $1,000 Caruso Award, and has appeared many times since as a Metropolitan Opera star—none other than leading bass soloist Jerome Hines.

Persistence in salesmanship pays off. One poll found that 90% of salespeople did not return to a potential customer after the third contact, but 80% of sales were made after the fifth contact.[14]

"You are the fifth insurance salesman that has tried to see me today," said the president of a large company. It was five o'clock and the salesman had just succeeded in selling the president a substantial policy. "You ought to feel gratified that you are the one who succeeded in selling me," the president added. Replied the insurance salesman, "Sir, I am all five of them!"

We admire the iron man of baseball, Cal Ripken Jr., for his record of 2,632 consecutive games played in the major leagues. All-time major league leader in hitting home runs is Hank Aaron with 755. In second place, Babe Ruth, Sultan of Swat, has a lifetime record of 714. It often goes unnoticed that Babe Ruth owned the strikeout record of 1,130 times as well. He reputedly said to his coach, "In a slump, I know that

I'm much closer to the one I'll hit out of the park."

Lance Armstrong, a winning bike rider, was twenty-four when diagnosed with testicular, lung, and brain cancer. He overcame his illnesses and unbelievably fought his way back to win six straight grueling European Tour de France championships. (The Tour de France lasts three weeks and has been likened to running a marathon every day for twenty consecutive days.)

Winning football coach Vince Lombardi said, "The real glory is being knocked to your knees and then coming back." No one experienced this more than Thomas Edison. He reportedly tried 1,000 times to make the light bulb before he finally succeeded.

BIBLICAL EXAMPLES OF PERSEVERANCE

After the Israelites had successfully passed through the Red Sea, well on their way to the promised land, twelve spies were chosen to case out the anticipated territory. On return from their secret exploration they reported that the land did indeed flow with milk and honey, and brought back samples of its abundant, enviable fruit. But ten of them, intimidated by its powerful giants and large, fortified cities, discouraged the Israelites from trying to capture Canaan. The other two spies, Joshua and Caleb, argued for ignoring the majority report, moving forward and attacking the enemy, reminding the people of God's previous victories over their enemies, and his ever-present strength to help as he had in the past.

But the people heeded the ten, became disheartened, and refused to keep on. As a result an entire generation wandered in the wilderness for forty years and perished without setting foot in their rightful heritage. But Joshua and Caleb, who did not lose heart but insisted they should go forward, trusting God, were the only two adults to enjoy entrance into the promised land.

Five years after Joshua had conquered much of Canaan, Caleb came to Joshua with a request:

> "I was forty years old when Moses the servant of the Lord sent me from Kadesh Barnea to explore the land. And I brought him back a report according to my convictions, but my brothers who went up with me made the hearts of the people melt with fear. I, however, followed the Lord my God wholeheartedly....
>
> "Now then, just as the Lord promised, he has kept me alive for forty-five years since the time he said this to Moses... So, here I am today, eighty-five years old! I am still as strong today as the day Moses sent me out; I'm just as vigorous to go out to battle now as I was then. Now give me this hill country that the Lord promised me that day. You yourself heard then that the Anakites were there and their cities were large and fortified, but the Lord helping me, I will drive them out just as he said" (Josh. 14:7-12).

Then Joshua blessed Caleb and gave him the area of Hebron, which Caleb proceeded to conquer, including the giants. Caleb had certainly kept on keeping on for over eight decades. The Lord always exhorted his commanders to be strong and take courage.

Despite temporary lapses during their days with Jesus, the post-resurrection apostles were not a discouraged group. Rather, to read the book of Acts is to follow the story of a band who, in the face of opposition, persecution, and ultimate martyrdom for most, radiated optimism, enthusiasm, and joy as they persevered to victory, carrying the gospel to much of the Roman Empire.

Paul exemplified faithfulness, continuance, and steadfastness. In the midst of human oppression and Satanic opposition, he was always able to affirm his faith in God. At the end of his life he could say, "I have fought the good fight, I have finished the race, I have kept the faith" (2 Tim. 4:7).

MISSIONARY PERSEVERANCE

David Brainerd, pioneer missionary among New England Indians, persisted in the path of duty during the darkest and toughest of circumstances. He wrote in his journal, "I had very little reason to hope that God had made me instrumental in the conversion of any of the Indians except my interpreter and his wife. I began to entertain thoughts of giving up my mission at the conclusion of the present year. I did so purely through dejection of spirit, pressing discouragement. Just as I lost heart came revival."

RESOLVE GETS GOD'S WORK DONE

What we need in all crises of life is an overwhelming determination to stick it out. On January 17, 2002, the nation's leading media organizations, including CNN, AP, CBS, NBC and ABC, among others, converged at Helen Hayes Rehabilitation Hospital, just forty miles north of New York City, for a news conference announcing the discharge of the last survivor pulled alive from the World Trade Center disaster. Port Authority Police Sergeant John McLoughlin had been buried under thirty feet of debris, pinned in a cavern "the size of a body" when the first tower collapsed on 9/11. Twenty-two hours later he was extricated by rescuers who dug him out by hand, and taken to Bellevue Hospital in critical condition. He sustained respiratory and kidney failure and needed twenty-six surgeries to repair skin and tissue damage before admittance to Helen Hayes Hospital for rehabilitation.

At first he could neither walk nor sit up, yet therapists credited him as one of the most motivated patients with whom they had ever worked. Vigorous therapy, the encouragement of his family, and the many cards from friends across the country fired up his all-consuming resolve to regain mobility and return home to his family. His four-year-old daughter sat on his lap during the interview. Responding to a reporter's question as to what he would tell others in desperate circumstances, he did not hesitate. "Don't give up. There is always hope." Since his discharge he has continued outpatient rehabilitation, and little by little he's coming closer to his goal.

In his valedictorian address in May 1999 at his Birmingham, Alabama, high school, senior Ben Talmadge reported the experience of an African pastor surrounded by rebels who demanded that he renounce his faith. He refused. The night before they took his life, he wrote his long-time philosophy of life and resolve in these lines on a scrap of paper:

> "I am part of the 'Fellowship of the Unashamed.' I have Holy Spirit power. The die has been cast. I've stepped over the line. The decision has been made. I am a disciple of his [Jesus]. I won't look back, let up, slow down, back away or be still. My past is redeemed, my present makes sense, and my future is secure. I am finished and done with low living, sight walking,

small planning, smooth knees, colorless dreams, tame visions, mundane talking, chintzy giving and dwarfed goals!

"I no longer need preeminence, prosperity, position, promotions, plaudits, or popularity. I don't have to be right, first, tops, recognized, praised, regarded or rewarded. I now live by presence, lean by faith, love by patience, lift by prayer and labor by power. My face is set, my gait is fast, my goal is Heaven, my road is narrow, my way is rough, my companions few, my guide reliable, my mission clear. I cannot be bought, compromised, detoured, lured away, turned back, diluted or delayed. I will not flinch in the face of sacrifice, hesitate in the presence of adversity, negotiate at the table of the enemy, ponder at the pool of popularity, or meander in the maze of mediocrity.

"I won't give up, shut up, let up, or burn up until I've preached up, prayed up, paid up, stored up and stayed up for the cause of Christ.

"I am a disciple of Jesus. I must go till he comes, give till I drop, preach till all know and work till he stops.

"And when he comes to get his own, he'll have no problem recognizing me. My colors will be clear."[15]

On May 27, 2001, New Tribes Mission American missionaries Martin and Grace Burnham were kidnapped from a Philippine island beach, where they were celebrating their eighteenth wedding anniversary. After more than a year of harrowing captivity, a firefight erupted when Philippine armed forces attempted to rescue the hostages in a surprise raid on June 7, 2002. Grace Burnham was resting in a hammock when a bullet ripped through her thigh and sent her rolling down a hill. She discovered her husband slumped nearby fatally wounded, blood gushing from his chest. A Philippine nurse, a loyal friend, also lost her life.

On the following Sunday a memorial service was held in Manila at the same time Grace was undergoing surgery for the gunshot wound. According to the New Tribes Mission field director who spoke at the memorial service, the last thing the couple did before the raid was pray together. Martin Burnham told his wife, "We might not leave this jungle alive, but at least we can leave this world serving the Lord with gladness. We can serve him right here where we are, and with gladness."

John Wesley, at age 82, wrote this entry in his *Journal* (January 4, 1785): "At this season (New Year) we usually distribute coal and bread among the poor of the Society. But now I considered, and they wanted clothes as well as food. So on this day and four following days I walked through the town and begged two hundred pounds in order to clothe them that needed it most. But it was hard work as most of the streets were filled with melting snow, which often lay ankle-deep, so that my feet were steeped in snow water nearly from morning till evening. I held out pretty well till Saturday evening; but I was laid up with a violent flux, which increased every hour until, at six in the morning, Dr. Whitehead called upon me."

What a challenge! Wesley, in his 80s, still following his rule of conduct:

> Do all the good you can,
> In all the ways you can,
> In all places you can,

Keep On Keeping On

At all times you can,
To all the people you can,
As long as ever you can.

Keep on keeping on!

Chapter 8

How to Keep From Quitting

Before his marriage, Oswald Chambers and his fiancée had a dream of partnership in producing books. Biddy, proficient in shorthand (250 words a minute), would take his sermons down and then transcribe them. During the seven years of their married life, their duties gave little time for a writing ministry, but wherever her husband was speaking her pencil flew over the pages of her stenographer's notebook.

In 1917 Chambers died unexpectedly at 43. Biddy did not forget the dream of her husband's book ministry. After three years of meticulously transcribing hundreds of talks from her storehouse of shorthand notes, she compiled a 365-page daily devotional, one of the most influential books of all times—*My Utmost For His Highest.* Nowhere in the book did she mention her own name nor her painstaking labor. To her the author was Oswald Chambers. She was only the channel of conveyance.

Before she died in 1966, fifty books had been published under her husband's name. Today his works are read by millions in scores of languages round the world, all because she didn't quit, but kept on investing long hours at her typewriter to produce yet another book.[16]

Another major law of sowing and reaping is this: *We gath-*

er a full harvest only if we persevere and do not quit. The harvest never comes on its own. Weeds grow by themselves, but crops require cultivation. When the going gets tough and weariness dogs our path, how do we defeat discouragement and keep from quitting?

(1) By talking to ourselves. On waking, or just before retiring, or during the day, your disheartened self says to you, "Things aren't going so well, are they? You've certainly got problems." Immediately, instead of agreeing and commiserating with your self-pity, you must take your life in your hand and talk to your discouraged soul. That's what the psalmist David did. He asked, "Why are you downcast, O my soul? Why so disturbed within me?" Then David spoke again to his soul, "Put your hope in God, for I will yet praise him, my Savior and my God" (Ps. 42:5-6).

Apparently David did this often (42:11; 43:5). Whenever his soul depressed him, he spoke up, "Soul, listen. I wish to speak to you. What right have you to be disquieted?" He turned on himself, and exhorted himself, "Put your hope in God."

In his fugitive days before he became a king, David had to face many disturbing situations. Once, when he and his army returned from a battle, they found their headquarters burned and their wives and children gone, taken away captive. The record says, "David was greatly distressed because the men were talking of stoning him; each one was bitter in spirit because of his sons and daughters." Instead of running or giving up, defeated, David talked to himself and to God. The Scripture tells us, "David found strength in the Lord his God" (1 Sam. 30:3-6).

That's what we must do. Instead of complaining, dejected

and defeated, we need to preach to ourselves, rebuke ourselves, encourage ourselves, say to ourselves, "Put your hope in God." Remind ourselves that God is all-powerful, all-loving, and ever-faithful. And remember how much he has helped us and what he has promised to do in our lives. Remember, we serve a mighty God. Sing a hymn of encouragement like *How Great Thou Art*, and keep on singing and then keep on keeping on.

(2) By prayer. Jesus told a parable to his disciples "to show them that they should always pray and not give up" (Lk. 18:1). Jesus' juxtaposition of prayer and quitting seems to indicate their mutual exclusiveness. If one is praying, he's less likely to be quitting. If one is thinking of quitting, he needs to pray.

A teenager became the favorite baby-sitter and close friend of a family of seven children, all girls. The sisters soon became aware of their baby-sitter's heart's desire to someday marry. Heading her Christmas list every year was this request, "A Christian husband." It was a desire, not an obsession. She graduated from nursing school and rose to the position of supervisor at a psychiatric center for mentally disturbed teenagers, lavishing them with homemade brownies and elaborately decorated parties. At the same time she was a leader for teenage girls at her church. She traveled, dated, but no Christian husband.

She and the sisters kept praying. The years went by. As her mother's health declined, she devoted more and more of her time to household duties and the care of her mother. When her mother died and her father became ill, she resigned her job after twenty years of service to become his full-time caretaker. It occurred to her that this devotion might permanently end her quest for a husband, but she never stopped praying.

Before long a man in her church, a widower of comfortable means who observed her tender care of her parents and admired her joyful spirit, asked her to marry him. Together they entertained missionaries, and served their church in many ways. Both gave much to each other and to others. Despite their age difference they had seventeen rich years together. The baby-sitter had patiently kept on through the years, delighting herself in the Lord who gave her the desires of her heart.

The Lord "gives strength to the weary and increases the power of the weak. Even youths grow tired and weary, and young men stumble and fall; but those who hope in the Lord will renew their strength. They will soar on wings like eagles; they will run and not grow weary, they will walk and not be faint" (Is. 40:29-31).

We ought always to pray and not to quit. To pray helps to stay!

(3) By self-discipline. Paul was familiar with the Isthmian games held every two years near Corinth. Athletes trained ten months in advance, disciplining themselves by giving up anything that might prevent them from winning. Paul was in a far greater contest. He wrote, "Everyone who competes in the games goes into strict training. They do it to get a crown that will not last; but we do it to get a crown that will last forever. Therefore I do not run like a man running aimlessly; I do not fight like a man beating the air. No, I beat my body and make it my slave so that after I have preached to others, I myself will not be disqualified for the prize" (1 Cor. 9:25-27).

The Old Testament contains many stories of leaders who in later life were tripped up by pride or lust. They failed to exercise self-control. In the hour of temptation our faithful

God has promised to provide a way of escape in each case (1 Cor. 10:13). Available to every believer is the inner strength of the Holy Spirit. He gives us power to stay close to Christ and to keep from quitting.

(4) By listening to the encouragement of others. The Lord told Moses to encourage his assistant Joshua to lead Israel into the promised land (Deut. 1:38). In the battle at Gibeah near the end of the era of the judges, the men of Israel encouraged one another (Judg. 20:22). When godly King Josiah celebrated a special Passover after Hilkiah the priest found the Book of the Law in the temple (2 Chr. 34:14-15), he not only removed all the idols from the land of Judah, but he "appointed the priests to their duties and encouraged them in the service of the Lord's temple" (2 Chr. 34:33-35:2). In every case the encouragement helped God's people stay the course.

For years William Wilberforce, philanthropist and member of Britain's parliament, had pressed for the abolition of slavery. Discouraged, he was thinking of giving up. His friend, John Wesley, learned of it on his deathbed and wrote with shaking hand, "If God be for you, who can be against you? Oh be not weary of well-doing! Go on, in the name of God and in the power of his might, till even American slavery shall vanish away before it." Wesley died six days later, but Wilberforce battled 45 more years until 1833, just before his own death, he witnessed the abolition of slavery in Britain.

Believers are specifically commanded to encourage each other to good works. "Let us consider how we may spur one another on toward love and good deeds" (Heb. 10:24). The next verse suggests a vital, indispensable place for mutual support—the church service. "Let us not give up meeting together, as some are in the habit of doing, but let us encourage one another—and all the more as you see the Day approaching" (v. 25). In the assembly believers cheer each other in hymns and spiritual songs, in testimonies, by the reading of Scripture, through public prayers and the teaching and preaching of the leaders.

Note the mutuality. Not only are we to be the recipients of exhortations from fellow believers, but we in turn are to instill hope and incite inspiration in others. Everyone needs encouragement from time to time, and we may be the Lord's chosen vessel to bring that elevation of enthusiasm.

(5) By cultivating patience in God's waiting room. Paul wrote that "suffering produces perseverance" (Rom. 5:3). Delay in waiting for God to act, whether in sending a harvest or righting a wrong, may be a form of suffering. When Joseph was sent to prison for a crime he didn't commit, he became a perfect candidate for anger, revenge, self-pity, and discouragement (Gen. 39:6-21). When would God release him and vindicate his innocence? But Joseph chose patience, waited for God to act, and in the meantime sharpened his administrative skills. In time Joseph was released from prison and elevated to second-in-command and enjoyed a productive leadership during Egypt's seven-year famine.

Though the Lord promised the throne of Israel to David, he must have wondered many times if he would ever reign, for Saul made attempt after attempt to assassinate him. But the tables turned, and twice David had the opportunity to end Saul's life. In both cases David declined to lift his hand against the Lord's anointed, choosing to wait out God's time and God's way for ending Saul's life, and placing David on the throne. Through patience David prevailed.

When the harvest is delayed, we must avoid the tendency

to slow down and become apathetic. Rather, we should remember that all things work together for good in God's great purpose. Pressures and problems in the waiting room of God's schooling, instead of separating us from the love of God, are meant to make us to become more than conquerors.

If you seem to be in a passageway that's black as night, take heart, for it may be a shortcut tunnel to the light. Patience takes the bricks that are thrown at us to build a solid foundation for a better life.

A seminary student worked for a construction company during his summer vacation. When the foreman learned that his new crewmember was the local preacher's son, he was determined to break him. That summer he cursed the lad, criticized his work without reason, made him tear out a job and do it over for no purpose, and even kicked him on more than one occasion. Many days the boy came home saying, "Dad, I don't think I can take another day." His father would pray with him, and encourage him to stick it out. A few months later, guess who walked in the church door to visit a service? Later that same foreman professed Christ as his savior.

James wrote, "Consider it pure joy, my brothers, whenever you face trials of many kinds, because you know that the testing of your faith develops perseverance. Perseverance must finish its work so that you may be mature and complete, not lacking anything" (1:2-4).

(6) By pondering our glorious future. Our greatest joys in this life are but a tantalizing foretaste of the eternal joys that await us. We need to anticipate the glories gleaming beyond the sunset. The wonders ahead that God is preparing for us are unimaginably beyond description. Try to realize, in some small degree at least, the magnificence of the place to which

we are headed. That is part of the cure for withstanding the difficulties and delays of the harvest. Was not Jesus enabled to endure the cross because of the joy set before him? (Heb. 12:2). Remember—the crowning day is coming!

Such expectation motivated the apostle Paul to bear up under his heavy and endless trials. He wrote, "Therefore we do not lose heart. Though outwardly we are wasting away, yet inwardly we are being renewed day by day. For our light and momentary troubles are achieving for us an eternal glory that far outweighs them all. So we fix our eyes not on what is seen, but on what is unseen. For what is seen is temporary, but what is unseen is eternal" (2 Cor. 4:16-18)

Paul was saying, "It will be worth it all."

PRIZES AND SURPRISES

One preacher commented, "At the judgment seat of Christ when awards are given, some will receive real prizes. And many will get surprises."

Rev. Leymon (Deak) Ketcham, former vice-president of The Kings College, and later Director of Development at Gordon College, and a dear friend of mine, learned he had terminal cancer at age fifty-one. From his hospital bed in his final days he wrote,

> "The Lord has allowed me to have a little glimpse of what my life and ministry has meant to a few people back through the years. This experience has brought me great joy of heart to know that I have not labored in vain. I have received letters by the score from people who were either saved through the preaching of the Word, or who were helped and

blessed in some way. Many times I did not know that my life was any kind of challenge to them. Of course, when we get to heaven we will find out completely the story of what our lives have meant and how they have been invested, for the Lord keeps the books."

Jesus taught of a future judgment in which the King separates the sheep from the goats, then says to his sheep, "Come, you who are blessed by my Father; take your inheritance.... For I was hungry, and you gave me something to eat, I was thirsty and you gave me something to drink, I was a stranger and you invited me in, I needed clothes and you clothed me, I was sick and you looked after me, I was in prison and you came to visit me" (Matt. 25:34-36). At this point those rewarded are puzzled as to when they did all these things. They have a hard time remembering those occasions. They are surprised!

So they ask him when they did all those things. The Lord replies, "Whatever you did for one of the least of these brothers of mine, you did for me" (Matt. 25:40). Back in this life, whenever the sheep extended their kindness to any member of the Lord's family, they were doing it to the Lord. They hadn't realized it at the time, but they had performed a good deed that the Lord of the harvest had noticed, and for which they were now being made aware, and receiving honorable recognition and reward. And they do so with great surprise, even astonishment. (The converse should be noted—that those on the left side, the goats, also experienced surprise at their failure to take advantage of opportunities to do good.)

In that future day many faithful saints are in for a most pleasant surprise when the Lord reveals how our lives touched other lives, all unknown to us, helping them to become a Christian, or overcome temptation, or take a step forward in the Christian life, or see them through a rough time. Dedicated Sunday school teachers, church officers, pastors, missionaries, and loyal followers of Christ will be full of joy at disclosures of how God worked through them. How exciting it will be to find someone there who tells us that we were the reason they're now in heaven. A missionary prayer calendar (Nov. 2001) quotes Henry Brooks Adams: "A teacher affects eternity; he can never tell where his influence stops."

The unsung faithful will be honored. Many, counted among the Christians' *Who's Who* down here, may not be listed in the heavenly *Who's Who* up there. Some crossroads country pastor who faithfully shepherded his flock and went to his grave unheralded may outshine Billy Graham up there, and some unnoticed missionary be more revered than the famous Livingstone. Some who sat on pulpit chairs may fade into the background, while quiet, dedicated pew-sitters get top seats. Many, low on the totem pole of Christian organizations, may be elevated to higher status.

A legend tells of an angel who at the start of a new church construction announced that he would award a prize to the person who made the most significant contribution to the finished product. Who would win—the architect, the contractor, the craftsman in glass, the sculptor of lovely statuary, or the carpenter assigned the fancy woodwork? All worked hard. What a surprise when the winner turned out to be an elderly peasant woman who every day carried hay to the ox that pulled the stones for the stonecutters!

Some day Jesus' "Well done" will fall on the ears of many whom others dubbed failures, fulfilling Jesus' prediction,

"Many who are first will be last, and many who are last will be first" (Matt. 19:30).

Ray Boltz's song, *Thank You,* imagines a man meeting his old Sunday school teacher up in heaven and letting him know for the first time how he had bowed his head during class one Sunday morning back on earth and received Jesus as his Savior. Another line relates several people from various nations approaching him to explain how giving to missionaries made it possible for them to hear the gospel. "Thank you," they said, "I'm so glad you gave."

During World War II a high schooler from Sheboygan, Wisconsin, and two pals were visiting a USO center in Chicago on a Saturday evening. A volunteer worker walked up to them, explained the gospel, and asked if they would like to make a decision for Christ. Told to bow their heads, they were supposed to pray as the worker led them. Not fully understanding the gospel, and not used to praying, all three of the boys peeked through their fingers and spotted each other peeking. Unable to restrain themselves, they burst into laughter and ran from the building.

A year later the same high schooler was listening to a guest speaker in his hometown, the well-known youth evangelist Jack Wyrtzen. As he listened, the high schooler kept thinking, "That's what that fellow back in the Chicago USO told us." The high schooler became a Christian and later received a call to the ministry, becoming the pastor of a large evangelical church in the East. The USO volunteer never knew it. To his death he probably remembered his failed attempt that night to witness to these boys and how they ran out of the building. He likely considered the affair a complete fiasco and became discouraged whenever he thought of it. What a surprise he's in for when in heaven he meets the high schooler and learns of his share in the conversion of this boy who became a pastor.

This petition appears in the *Book of Common Prayer* (the Sunday next before Advent): "Stir up, we beseech thee, O Lord, the wills of thy faithful people; that they, plenteously bringing forth the fruit of good works, may of thee be plenteously rewarded; through Jesus Christ our Lord. Amen."

> Who does God's work will get God's pay,
> However long may seem the day,
> However weary be the way.
> God hurries not, nor makes delay,
> Who works for him will get his pay,
> Some certain hour, some certain day.
> No mortal hand, God's hand can stay.
> He does not pay as others pay
> In gold or land or raiment gay,
> In goods that perish and decay.
> But God's high wisdom knows a way
> And this is sure, let come what may,
> Who does God's work, will get God's pay."
>
> —Anonymous

Don't let anyone or any failed work keep you from persevering. The needs are great and the rewards are certain.

Stay faithful to our great God in your service to Christ.

Keep on keeping on.

Notes

1. Richard J. Mouw, *He Shines in All That's Fair* (Grand Rapids, MI: Wm. B. Eerdmans Publishing Co., 2001), pp. 38-39.

2. August 12, 2002, p. 51.

3. C.S. Lewis, "Good Work and Good Works" in *The World's Last Night and Other Essays* (New York: Harcourt, Brace, Jovanovich, Inc, 1960), p. 71.

4. Patricia Cornwell, *Ruth, A Portrait,* (New York: Doubleday, 1997), p.178.

5. Mathew Woodly, "Where is Jesus Today?", *Decision,* June 2002.

6. Reprinted from *How To Overcome Discouragement* by Armin R. Gesswein, copyright 1991 by Christian Publications, Inc. Used by permission of Christian Publications, Inc., 800-233-4443.

7. David McCullough, *Truman* (New York: Touchstone, 1992), p. 95.

8. Julie B. Sevig, "Refugee Says Thanks." Reprinted by permission from the December 2000 issue of *The Lutheran*, 37, copyright 2000, Augsburg Press.

9. *Jews for Jesus Newsletter*, "A Message from Moishe."

10. Letter from Prison Fellowship Ministries, June 2000.

11. James F. Engel and H. Wilbert Norton, *What's Gone Wrong With The Harvest?* (Grand Rapids, MI: Zondervan Publishing Company, 1975), p. 45.

12. *Jews for Jesus Newsletter*, "A Message from Moishe."

13. Quoted in Charles W. Shedd, *Time for All Things* (Nashville: Abingdon Press, 1962), p. 44.

14. *Decision*, July 2000.

15. Reprinted from *Alliance Life*, September 2000, permission of Ben Talmadge.

16. David McCasland, *Oswald Chambers: Abandoned To God* (Grand Rapids, MI: Discovery House Publishers, 1993).

*O*ther great books by Leslie B. Flynn!

What the Church Owes the Jew
~Leslie B. Flynn

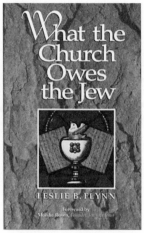

What do you know about the unique Jewish contribution to the Scriptures, the Church, and to the world at-large? Dr. Leslie Flynn, who served as pastor to many Jewish Christians in the New York area, passionately shares these answers and more (e.g., anti-Semitism, the Jewishness of Jesus), to help Jews and non-Jews build bridges of understanding and friendship.
ISBN 0-9654806-3-1 paper $12.00

Jesus in the Image of God:
A Challenge to Christlikeness
~Leslie B. Flynn

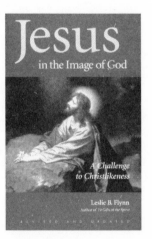

A great book for Bible study groups! Here's a real antidote to the negative and faithless views of the Jesus Seminar. Let the Jesus of the Gospels challenge you to become more like him—the Son of God created in God's own image, who overcame despair, sorrow, rejection, and humiliation to bring healing, redemption, hope, and the Good News of God's love to all human beings.
ISBN 0-9654806-1-5 paper $12.00

Available at your favorite bookstore
or call **1-800-463-7818** • Major credit cards accepted
Magnus Press, P.O. Box 2666, Carlsbad, CA 92018

Call today for 25% discount on all books!